PLAUTUS'
MENAECHMI

Other Titles by Gilbert Lawall
Published by Bolchazy-Carducci Publishers, Inc.

Petronius: Selections from the Satyricon
xvi + 260 pp. (1975, 1978, Second ed. 1980, Reprint 1982, 1987, 1989,
   Third ed. 1995, Reprint 1997, 2002, 2004)
   Paperback, ISBN 0-86516-288-3

The Phaedra of Seneca
with Sarah Lawall and Gerda Kunkel
Illus., 238 pp. (1982, Reprint 1989, Revised 1995, Reprint 1997, 2004)
   Paperback, ISBN 0-86516-016-3

Twelfth Printing, 2012

Bolchazy-Carducci Publishers, Inc.
1570 Baskin Road
Mundelein, Illinois 60060
www.bolchazy.com

Printed in the United States of America
2012
by CreateSpace

ISBN 978-0-86516-007-1

PLAUTUS'
MENAECHMI

EDITED WITH INTRODUCTION
AND RUNNING VOCABULARIES BY

GILBERT LAWALL AND **BETTY NYE QUINN**

with the help of
Eugenie Fawcett • Paul Hamilton
James Salisbury • Barbara Young
Sally Washam

1st edition: 1978
2nd edition: 1980

Bolchazy-Carducci Publishers, Inc.
Mundelein, Illinois USA

PREFACE

This book is intended for use in second or third year high school Latin classes and in second or third semester college Latin courses. The presence of facing vocabularies makes the book ideal for sight translation. Teachers should take full advantage of the possibilities of dramatizing scenes or the entire play.

The material for the running vocabularies and stage directions was assembled by undergraduate and graduate students in a course in Roman drama taught in the spring of 1977 at the University of Massachusetts at Amherst by Professor Gilbert Lawall. The following students contributed material: Eugenie Fawcett, Paul Hamilton, James Salisbury, Barbara Young, and Sally Washam. Material for the Introduction was prepared by Professor Betty Nye Quinn of Mount Holyoke College, who also helped with the final editing of stage directions and running vocabularies and wrote the study questions. The entire book was retyped with corrections and additions in 1980.

INTRODUCTION

PLAUTUS AND HIS AGE

The comedies of Titus Maccius Plautus (ca. 254 - 184 B.C.) belong to a period of Rome's dynamic expansion and broadening horizons -- international, economic, political, social, and cultural. By the end of the third century B.C., Rome had emerged from victorious wars with Pyrrhus and with Carthage as the dominant power in the western Mediterranean and was already beginning to play what was to become a major role in eastern affairs. The foundations of empire had been laid in the acquisition of Sicily, Sardinia, Corsica, Spain, and a tiny protectorate in Illyricum (across the Adriatic). Meanwhile, Roman armies and subsequent military colonies were extending Roman power into the Gallic wilderness of northern Italy. The second century brought a preoccupation with Greece and the Hellenistic monarchies of the East. Attention was focused on Greece out of an irrational fear of the East and out of an idealistic devotion to the idea of Greek liberty; the Romans feared for Rome itself because of the capriciousness of Greek internal politics and because of the constant dabbling of Hellenistic monarchs therein, and they firmly proclaimed and fought for the ideal of freedom for Greek cities in Greece proper and in Asia Minor. Before Plautus' death, Roman soldiers had campaigned through Greece to defeat Philip of Macedon in two wars and in 189 crossed the Aegean to defeat Antiochus the Great, king of the Seleucid empire in Syria, at Magnesia (in modern Turkey).

Economically the state was prospering as never before. Tax revenues from these initial provinces, war debts from allies and defeated enemies, war booty and spoils, and increased commercial ventures enabled a rapid recovery from the devastation of resources suffered from the fifteen year occupation of Italy by Hannibal's ravaging Carthaginians in the Second Punic War. So solvent was the treasury that citizens were given partial repayment of the extraordinary war tax levied in that war. Before the middle of the second century, direct taxation of Roman citizens was to be abolished, since revenues from other sources were sufficient to meet the needs of government.

Domestic politics were dominated by foreign affairs, since the concerns of government were almost exclusively those of defense: protection of the borders, aid to allies, and punitive actions. During Plautus' active career, the most influential man in Rome was P. Cornelius Scipio Africanus, the conqueror of Hannibal, whose life span almost parallels that of the dramatist. Scipio and his political adherents were philhellenes and active internationalists, supporting foreign wars and the expansion of Roman influence. Their political opponents, whom we may conveniently group under the name of their standard bearer, the doughty Cato the Censor, pursued a more isolationist line, eschewing foreign ventures unless suggestive of monetary or territorial advantages and evincing no sentimental attachment for the vanished glories of Greece.

Several new elements were appearing in the Roman social fabric. The numbers and importance of wealthy businessmen had increased through the logistical demands of the Second Punic War and subsequent campaigns, the foundation of tax farming investment companies for the provincial revenues, and widening commercial opportunities. More and more slaves were available through foreign conquest, and, more importantly, highly educated slaves were being imported from the East. In addition, many more foreigners of every trade and profession were making their way to Rome for personal economic reasons or in the diplomatic service of their states.

The Romans, who had been for some four and a half centuries relatively isolated from the rest of the world, had nurtured and passed on an ordered society, structured within the traditions of their forefathers, based on respect for the authority of the gods, the state, and the family, and emphasizing the qualities of courage, patriotism, seriousness, industry, frugality, and temperance, and assuming a rigid moral code in regard to familial and sexual relationships. Adultery, extra-marital affairs, divorce, and homosexuality were, if practiced, rarely publicized, and if known, caused scandal and disgrace and were likely to be associated with non-Romans, foreigners, i.e., Greeks.

Whatever Greek influence can be found in earlier Roman history, there is no doubt that from the third century forward the Greek impact upon Roman life was enormous, lasting, and welcomed by an influential majority of all classes. No people have ever admired and accepted Greek norms of excellence more than the Romans, and none have been more frank in admitting and even bragging that they followed the Greeks in the arts and in matters of the mind. As they entered the international sphere where Greek was the language of diplomacy and Greek culture was the hallmark of civilization, the Romans quickly assimilated and adapted the refinements of a people to whose military and political efficiency they were vastly superior.

ANCIENT COMEDY AND THE ROMAN STAGE

Probably every primitive people develops early in its history some kind of nascent drama, usually in connection with worship of the gods and religious festivals. To this pattern the Romans were no exception. We hear of rude jesting at harvest festivals accompanied by music and dancing and of farces and mimes performed by professional actors at public games, but the specific details are muddled in our sources. Apparently these dramatic representations featured buffoonish stock characters embroiled in standard situations, and they relied on improvisation, crude wit, slapstick, and music for entertainment value.

Drama had presumably developed in some such way also among the early Greeks, but what the Romans met in southern Italy, Sicily, and Greece was a kind of urbane "comedy of manners," the latest in a series of three stages in the development of Greek comic drama, termed by literary critics, Old, Middle, and New Comedy. This continuing evolution of comedy reflects the changing political situation in Athens and in Greece. Old Comedy, known to us through nine extant plays of Aristophanes, is characterized by satirical attacks on contemporary political and social conditions and personalities and is a product of fifth century Athenian

democracy. The defeat of Athens in the Peloponnesian War, the political
shift from democracy to oligarchy under Spartan hegemony, and the conse-
quent diminution of individual political participation and of freedom of
speech caused dramatists to direct their satire against general human
foibles, such as greed and corruption, rather than against identifiable
individuals and programs. This transitional stage is known as Middle
Comedy and is represented for us by the *Ecclesiazusae* and *Plutus* of
Aristophanes.

When the importance of the individual Greek city states was overshadowed
by the conquests of Alexander and the rise of the Hellenistic monarchies
of his successors in Egypt and Asia Minor (late fourth and third centuries), dramatists turned to themes of everyday life among (generally)
well-to-do merchants and dealt with the normal problems arising in private
life, especially with the universal problems of love and marriage and the
conflicts between father and son in arranging a suitable match. Among the
many writers of this New Comedy known to us by name, only Menander (343 -
291 B.C.) is represented by any extant plays.

In 241 B.C. the Romans achieved victory over Carthage in the First Punic
War, thus humbling one of the great powers of the Mediterranean, defeating
a naval empire by building their own fleet and carrying the war to Africa
and Sicily. Since this victory which catapulted Rome into the international limelight demanded a special celebration, officials decided to
bring to their citizens a sample of the regular entertainment to be found
in the Greek world. A receptive audience for this cultural innovation was
at hand among the soldiers who had campaigned in the Greek settlements of
southern Italy and Sicily and who had been exposed to art, architecture,
literature, and a way of life far more elegant and sophisticated than what
they had left at home. Accordingly, a comedy and a tragedy, modeled on
Greek originals, were presented at the *Ludi Romani* of 240 B.C. These
plays proved to be so successful that dramatic performances became a regular part of the *Ludi Romani* and during Plautus' active career were in-
cluded in several of the other public festivals in response to public demand.

These comedies, adapted from Greek originals, were called *fabulae
palliatae*, a name which denotes what to their contemporaries were their
distinguishing features: *fabulae*, "stories," because they had a written
plot, a text to be followed; *palliatae*, because they were acted in Greek
dress (the *palla*) in a Greek locale and with a Greek cast of characters.
The exotic note of this foreign *mise en scène* was enhanced both by the
status of the characters and by the attitudes and way of life presented.
Thus, wealthy merchants and their families, clever and impertinent slaves
in major and often starring roles, and professionals new to Roman life
(doctors, cooks, mercenary soldiers, and courtesans) strode the boards.
When slaves were sassy to their masters and actively intrigued against
them, when sons tricked and cheated their fathers out of money for love
affairs, and when the *pater familias* himself was made a gullible fool,
Romans could enjoy the joke with impunity, since these rowdies were after
all not Romans, but Greeks.

This Greek veneer, however, does not obscure the essential "Romanness" of the plays. Aside from the broad farcical episodes, occasional coarse jests and slapstick, which some scholars are, right or wrong, quick to attribute to Roman credit, there are unmistakeable allusions to contemporary politics (cf. *Menaechmi*, line 856), references to Roman laws and customs (571-95), and parodies of Roman tragedy (835ff.). Certainly also the dramatist has chosen to include historical (409-11), geographical (235-8), and mythological material (200-201), which may or may not have been in the original Greek version, but which is calculated to amuse his Roman audience and to amuse them in a way far different from the effect such allusions might have had for the Hellenistic audience. The emphasis upon obvious humor and entertainment value, rather than upon thoughtful social comment, and the lavish use of music make Plautine comedy distinctive from Greek New Comedy -- at least from the Menander which we have. A convenient, if inaccurate and fanciful, analogy might be Shaw's *Pygmalion* and the musical version, *My Fair Lady*.

The plays were performed as part of annual state festivals either within a temple precinct or on temporary stages erected for the festival; there was no permanent stone theatre in Rome until Pompey erected one in 55 B.C. It is not clear whether the spectators were supplied with seats or whether they stood; nor is it clear whether the actors wore masks.

The action of the plays was continuous, although to be sure the equation of dramatic and actual time sometimes strains credulity, e.g., in 882ff. where Senex reenters complaining that he has had to wait so long for Medicus, but he has in fact only been off stage for 5 verses.

The stage set is always the same (except for the *Rudens* which takes place on the coast of Africa): a city street running in front of three houses whose doors open directly on the street where all the action takes place. Sometimes only the residents of two houses are involved in the action (as in the *Menaechmi*), so the third house remains closed; occasionally one of the entrances is that of a temple instead of a residence (as in the *Curculio*). The exit to the spectators' right leads to the forum and that to the spectators' left to the harbor (and/or, in some plays, to the country). Thus Menaechmus II and his slave Messenio enter from the left (226), since they have just arrived at Epidamnus by sea, and Menaechmus I and Peniculus exit on the right (217), since they are going to the forum. Characters normally return from the place where they have gone.

Since there were no programs, the Roman dramatist had to deal with the problem of setting the stage, explaining the situation, and keeping the plot clear via verbal rather than written exposition. Consequently most plays have a prologue spoken sometimes by a minor deity and sometimes, as here, by an actor simply called Prologus. The first time a character appears, he usually identifies himself or is quickly identified by name or occupation by one of the others; there is a good deal of addressing people by name throughout. Identification of characters is also made clear by costume and properties. Thus, for example, a slave wears a red wig and a dark sleeveless tunic, an old man a white wig and a white *pallium* or cloak over his tunic, and a courtesan a red tunic and a saffron yellow *palla* or stole. Plautus has often been accused by modern critics of offering too much repetitious explanation, but, without the benefit of the fine acoustics of the Greek theatre, Roman dramatists had to make do with temporary facilities in which some key parts of the dialogue might be missed by a holiday crowd the first time important details were presented.

THE *MENAECHMI* AND ITS PLACE IN WESTERN COMIC DRAMA

Easily the best known of Plautus' plays, the *Menaechmi* is based on mistaken identities and eventual recognition. Whether the play represents an early endeavor of a novice or the finished product of an established playwright it is impossible to decide; it has been dated on the basis of various criteria as early as 215 B.C. and as late as 186.

The action of the play occurs in the town of Epidamnus (in western Greece) on the day on which the scion of a Sicilian merchant family arrives in search of his twin brother lost since childhood. The lost twin, kidnapped by a wealthy Epidamnian who adopted the child and left him his fortune, is now a man of importance in Epidamnus. The situation is further complicated by the fact that each twin bears the same name; the name of the kidnapped boy, Menaechmus, was given by his family to the surviving son, Sosicles, so we have Menaechmus I of Epidamnus and Menaechmus II (Sosicles) of Sicily. The visitor is mistaken for his brother by a succession of people, and the Epidamnian in turn is blamed for what the unknown visitor has said and done. Eventually, the situation is resolved when the twins meet fact to face. The plot is simple, develops out of itself, and offers innumerable opportunities for obvious humor.

The play's popularity has essentially rested on its broad farcical humor and exuberant dialogue. Few have been the critics who have found more than pure entertainment here. The carefully balanced structure of the alternating appearances of the brothers and the precision of the pattern of metrical variety have been studied. On the whole, however, its neat construction and the absence of any involved plot of intrigue (which is characteristic of several other Plautine plays, such as the *Epidicus* and the *Pseudolus*) have meant little attention to any deeper analysis. Erich Segal (*Roman Laughter*, Cambridge, 1968), who defines the purpose of Plautine comedy in general as providing a release from the normal routine of daily life, considers that the brothers represent "a conflict between holiday freedom and everyday restraint" (p. 43). A more ambitious interpretation has been advanced by Eleanor Winsor Leach (in *Arethusa* 2, 1969, p. 33) that the play symbolizes man's "seeking for a fully realized self," when the brothers, as "separated halves of one complete self," discover one another.

Since the Renaissance, various adaptations of the *Menaechmi* have appeared, but modern readers and playgoers will be most familiar with Shakespeare's *The Comedy of Errors*. Shakespeare transferred the scene to Ephesus (in modern Turkey) and made several additions: a second pair of twins, each a slave to one of the original twins; a love interest for the traveling brother, the sister of his brother's wife; the twins' father (long deceased in the *Menaechmi*), who is under penalty of death for disobeying the laws of Ephesus; and their missing mother who is finally reunited with her husband and family. Obviously here the opportunities for mistaken identities and farce have been increased, but Shakespeare has colored his blend of the romantic and the classic with an aura of mystery, magic, and near tragedy involving the twins' parents.

Shakespeare's play furnished the basis for the highly successful musical comedy, *The Boys from Syracuse* which opened in 1938 and was revived in 1963 when *A Funny Thing Happened on the Way to the Forum*, a masterful pastiche of Plautine plots and characters, was playing on Broadway. A favorite of summer and dinner theatres, *The Boys from Syracuse*, although twice removed from Plautus, provides for modern theatre goers that important dimension of music which so delighted the Roman audience.

It is probably safe to say that at least one performance of the *Menaechmi* occurs every year in some American college or university, a ready tribute to the enduring and universal appeal of Plautus' funniest farce which at its premiere aroused the laughter of the Roman veterans who had defeated Hannibal.

METRICS

The farcical situations, broad humor and quick repartee of the play can be readily enjoyed today. But what a modern reader can never appreciate is the effect on the original Roman audience of the music and varying meters of a Plautine production. Plautus' skill in a variety of musical rhythms is attested by his epitaph, whether or not composed by the poet himself:

> Postquam est mortem aptus Plautus...
> Et numeri innumeri simul omnes conlacrimarunt.

> After Plautus met his death, ... innumerable
> rhythms wept together in concert.

-Aulus Gellius, *Noctes Atticae* 1.23.3

The rhythms or meters used by Plautus may be divided into three main groups: DIALOGUE, RECITATIVE, and SONG. The meters of Roman poetry depend not on stress accent as in English verse, but on an alternation of long and short syllables. Spoken iambs ($\cup$ -) are used in the prologue, ordinary conversation, and especially for important exposition of the plot. The parts of the play written in iambics may conveniently be labeled DIALOGUE. Trochaics (- $\cup$) are used for animated and emotional conversation. The parts of the play written in trochaics are called RECITATIVE, and involved a different manner of delivery from the DIALOGUE sections. Finally, there are the lyric SONGS sung to the accompaniment of wind instruments. The meters used in the SONGS are very irregular and complex. The pattern of DIALOGUE, SONG, and RECITATIVE in the play is as follows:

Prologue	1-76	DIALOGUE
Act I	77-109	DIALOGUE
	110-134	SONG
	135-225	RECITATIVE

Act II	226-350	DIALOGUE
	351-368	SONG
	369-445	RECITATIVE
Act III	446-465	RECITATIVE
	466-558	DIALOGUE
Act IV	559-570	DIALOGUE
	571-603	SONG
	604-700	RECITATIVE
Act V	701-752	DIALOGUE
	753-774	SONG
	775-871	RECITATIVE
	872-881	DIALOGUE
Act VI	882-898	DIALOGUE
	899-965	RECITATIVE
	966-989	SONG
	990-1049	RECITATIVE
Act VII	1050-1162	RECITATIVE

These divisions will be marked in the text, and the reader should pay attention to the relationship between the dramatic structure of the play and the alternation of DIALOGUE, SONG, and RECITATIVE. For further discussion of meters and instructions on how to scan and read Plautus' Latin metrically, one may consult the books listed in the Bibliography. It is assumed by the editors that students in second or third year high school Latin or second or third semester college Latin (for whom this book is intended) will usually not be expected to attend to the complexities of Plautine scansion but will be content to read the Latin in its prose rhythms.

LANGUAGE

Some of the distinctive features of Plautus' language should be noted before the student begins to read the text. None should cause any serious trouble, and the running vocabularies will provide constant help in these matters.

   u is printed for both *u* and *v* throughout. Thus, *uobis* = *vobis* (2), *aduortite* = *advortite* (5), etc. *V* is printed for the capital *u* or *v*.

   o appears instead of *e* in the stems of some words: *aduortite* = *advertite* (5).

   u appears instead of *i* in some superlatives: *paucissuma* = *paucissima* (6).

-os (nominative) and *-om* (accusative) appear as the endings in second declension nouns and adjectives whose stems end in *u*: *auos* = *avus*; *seruos* = *servus*; *saluos* = *salvus*; *auom* = *avum*; *seruom* = *servum*; *saluom* = *salvum*.

-um (or *-om* after *u*) is used for the genitive plural *-orum*: *duom nummum* (542) = *duorum nummorum*.

med = *me* before a vowel.

ted = *te* before a vowel.

-ce or *-c* is frequently added to demonstrative pronouns: *hasce* = *has*; *hisce* = *hi* or *his*; *illic* = *ille*.

ipsus = *ipse*.

quoius = *cuius*.

quoi = *cui*.

qui = ablative (*quo*, *qua*, *quo*) or is used adverbially ("how," "why").

quom = *cum* (conj.).

-ier is used for the ending of the present passive infinitive: *flagitarier* (46) = *flagitari*.

siem = *sim* (subjunctive of *sum*).

duis = *des* (subjunctive of *do*).

faxo and *faxim* = subjunctive and optative of *facio*. *faxo* also = future or future perfect. *faxim* also = perfect subjunctive.

est is often elided with the previous word: 42 *domist* = *domi est*.

Future imperatives in *-to*, *-tote* are used frequently.

These and other features of Plautus' Latin will be noted in the facing vocabularies and need not be memorized now.

Vowels that are long by nature are marked in the text for convenience in reading the Latin aloud. Quantities are marked as in the *Oxford Latin Dictionary*. Those who wish to learn to read the Latin in its proper metrical patterns should consult the books listed in the Bibliography.

VOCABULARY

The vocabulary at the end of this book contains all words that occur in the play and are prescribed by the College Entrance Examination Board for the first two years of Latin. These words do not occur in the facing vocabularies. The facing vocabularies gloss all other words that occur in the play. After these words have occurred several times, they are marked with an asterisk and will not occur again in the facing vocabularies. They do appear in the vocabulary at the end of the book, where they are each marked with an asterisk.

BIBLIOGRAPHY

Allan G. Gillingham and Eric C. Baade, *Plautus for Reading and Production* (Scott, Foresman and Company, 1965, 1968). (Excellent introductory material on staging and costumes.)

Nicholas Moseley and Mason Hammond, ed., *T. Macci Plauti Menaechmi* (Harvard University Press, 1933). (The standard scholarly edition of the play. Contains material on metrics.)

P. Nison, tr., *Plautus II: Casina, The Casket Comedy, Curculio, Epidicus, the Two Menaechmuses* (Loeb Classical Library, Harvard University Press, 1965). (Bilingual edition.)

Erich Segal, *Roman Laughter: The Comedy of Plautus* (Harvard University Press, 1968).

Erich Segal, "The *Menaechmi*: Roman Comedy of Errors," *Yale Classical Studies* 21 (1969) 77-93.

Eleanor Winsor Leach, "MEAM QUOM FORMAM NOSCITO: Language and Characterization in the MENAECHMI," *Arethusa* 2 (1969) 30-45.

George Duckworth, *The Nature of Roman Comedy* (Princeton University Press, 1952).

DRAMATIS PERSONAE

PROLOGUS (PR.). prologue speaker.

PENICULUS (PE.). parasite of Menaechmus I.

MENAECHMUS I (ME.I). a gentleman living in Epidamnus.

EROTIUM (ER.). a courtesan in Epidamnus, mistress of Menaechmus I.

CYLINDRUS (CY.). Erotium's cook.

MENAECHMUS II (SOSICLES) (ME.II). a gentleman from Syracuse, twin
                                   brother of Menaechmus I.

MESSENIO (MES.). slave of Menaechmus II.

ANCILLA (AN.). maid of Erotium.

MATRONA (MA.). wife of Menaechmus I.

SENEX (SE.). father of Matrona.

MEDICUS (MED.). doctor.

LORARII (LO.). slaves.

ARGUMENTUM

1-76	Dialogue	PR.	Prologus tells the previous experiences of the two Menaechmi brothers.

ACT I

77-109	Dialogue	PE.	Peniculus comes to Menaechmus I's house in search of a free meal.
110-134	Song	ME.I, (PE.)	Menaechmus I comes out of his house with the stolen *palla* and is observed by Peniculus.
135-181	Recitative	ME.I, PE.	Menaechmus I and Peniculus meet and plan to go to Erotium's house for lunch and love.
182-217	Recitative	ME.I, PE., ER.	Menaechmus I gives Erotium the *palla* and asks her to prepare lunch to be ready when Peniculus and he return from the forum.
218-225	Recitative	ER., CY.	Erotium sends Cylindrus to market to buy provisions for lunch.

ACT II

226-272	Dialogue	ME.II, MES.	Menaechmus II and Messenio arrive from the harbor in search of Menaechmus II's long lost brother. Messenio gives Menaechmus II the *marsuppium* for safe keeping.
273-332	Dialogue	ME.II, MES., CY.	Cylindrus, returning from market with provisions for lunch, meets Menaechmus II and Messenio and mistakes Menaechmus II for Menaechmus I. Cylindrus goes in to cook lunch and to send Erotium out to invite Menaechmus in.
333-350	Dialogue	ME.II, MES.	Menaechmus II and Messenio puzzle over their reception in Epidamnus.
351-368	Song	ER., (ME.II, MES.)	Erotium invites Menaechmus II in for lunch.

369-431	Recitative	ER., ME.II, MES.	Erotium again invites Menaechmus II in for lunch. Menaechmus II hands the *marsuppium* to Messenio for safe keeping. Erotium asks Menaechmus II to take the *palla* to the embroiderer when he leaves. Menaechmus II promises to go in after talking to Messenio. Erotium exits.
432-441a	Recitative	ME.II, MES.	Menaechmus II sends Messenio toward the harbor to find an inn to stash the baggage and then to return to meet him before dark. Menaechmus II enters Erotium's house.
442b-445	Recitative	MES.	Messenio departs toward the harbor.

ACT III

446-465	Recitative	PE.	Peniculus, having lost track of Menaechmus I in the assembly, returns dejected, thinking that Menaechmus I sneaked back to Erotium's and has already finished the lunch. He sees Menaechmus II coming out of Erotium's house with a *corona*.
466-521	Dialogue	PE., ME.II.	Menaechmus II, carrying the *palla*, promises Erotium to take it to the embroiderer's and bring it back remade today. Peniculus, angry, vows to punish Menaechmus for lunching without him. Peniculus departs to tell all to Menaechmus I's wife.
522-548	Dialogue	ME.II, AN.	Ancilla gives Menaechmus II the *spinter* to be taken to the jeweler to be refashioned.
549-558	Dialogue	ME.II	Menaechmus II departs toward the harbor to rejoin Messenio; he throws the *corona* in the street leading to the forum.

ACT IV

559-570	Dialogue	MA., PE.	Matrona, having been informed by Peniculus of Menaechmus's doings, comes out and finds the *corona* in the street. Matrona and Peniculus see Menaechmus I returning from the forum, but without the *palla*.
571-603	Song	ME.I, (MA., PE.)	Menaechmus I, returning from the forum, sings a complaint about his client and about being late for his lunch with Erotium.
604-667	Recitative	ME.I, MA., PE.	Matrona upbraids Menaechmus I and makes him promise to get the *palla* back; she exits into her house; Peniculus, realizing he will get no favors from Matrona and none from Menaechmus, exits to the forum.
668-674	Recitative	ME.I	Shut out from his own house, Menaechmus I now goes to Erotium's house to get the *palla* back.
675-697	Recitative	ME.I, ER.	Menaechmus I asks Erotium for the *palla*; she says she has already given it to him and slams the door in his face.
698-700	Recitative	ME.I	Menaechmus I goes off to the forum to consult with his friends.

ACT V

701-752	Dialogue	ME.II, MA.	Menaechmus II could not find Messenio, and so he returns (still carrying the *palla*) and is met by Matrona. Menaechmus II denies he stole the *palla* from Matrona; she summons her father to defend her interests.
753-774	Song	SE., (ME.II, MA.)	Senex enters, complaining of old age and of quarrelsome wives.

775-852	Recitative	SE., ME.II, MA.	Senex lectures Matrona about be-ing a good wife and questions Menaechmus II, who pretends in-sanity in order to get rid of Matrona and Senex. He frightens off Matrona.
853-871	Recitative	SE., ME.II	The scene continues with Menaechmus II pretending to mount a chariot to attack and kill Senex; Menaechmus II col-lapses, apparently unconscious.
872-875	Dialogue	SE., ME.II	Senex, relieved, departs to fetch Medicus.
876-881	Dialogue	ME.II	Menaechmus II departs toward the harbor to return to his ship.

ACT VI

882-898	Dialogue	SE., MED.	Senex brings Medicus.
899-956	Recitative	ME.I, SE., MED.	Menaechmus I returns, complain-ing about Peniculus, who told all to Matrona. Medicus "diag-noses" Menaechmus' illness. Medicus orders Menaechmus to be taken to his office for treat-ment; Medicus departs; Senex de-parts to fetch slaves to carry Menaechmus to Medicus' office.
957-965	Recitative	ME.I	Menaechmus I, puzzled and shut out of both houses, sits down to wait for night.
966-989	Song	MES., (ME.I)	Messenio returns from the har-bor, having stashed the baggage, and comes to fetch Menaechmus II from Erotium's house. He sings a song about the "good" slave.
990-996	Recitative	SE., MES., ME.I, LO.	Senex brings the Lorarii to carry Menaechmus to Medicus' office.
997-1019	Recitative	MES., ME.I, LO.	Lorarii try to carry off Menaechmus I; Messenio comes to the rescue; they drive off the Lorarii.

| 1020-1038 | Recitative | MES., ME.I | Messenio asks for his freedom; Menaechmus I grants it. Messenio departs to harbor to fetch the *marsuppium*. |

| 1039-1049 | Recitative | ME.I | Menaechmus I, thoroughly confused, enters Erotium's house to beg her to return the *palla*. |

ACT VII

| 1050-1059 | Recitative | ME.II, MES. | Menaechmus II and Messenio, having met at the harbor, return. |

| 1060-1156 | Recitative | ME.I, ME.II, MES. | Menaechmus I enters from Erotium's house, denying that he took the *palla* and *spinter*. Then Messenio guides the brothers through the recognition scene. Menaechmus II has the *palla* and *spinter*. The two brothers depart into Menaechmus I's house. |

| 1157-1162 | Recitative | MES. | Messenio announces the auction of all Menaechmus I's property (including his wife) and asks for applause. |

1 principium, -ii, n. beginning.
   propitius, -a, -um. favorable, kind, propitious.
2 uobis = vobis
   spectator, -oris, m. a spectator.
3 apporto, 1. to bring.
   lingua, -ae, f. tongue, speech.
4 quaeso, -ere, -ii. to seek; to ask, beg.
   benignus, -a, -um. kind, friendly, favorable.
   auris, -is, f. ear.
5 argumentum, -i, n. subject, theme, argument.
   aduorto (adverto), -ere, -ti, -sum. to turn something toward a place.
     animum aduortere: to pay attention.
6 uerbum (verbum), -i, n. word.
   confero, -ferre, -tuli, collatum. to bring together, collect, gather
     (i.e., the *argumentum*).
   paucissuma = paucissima
7 poeta, -ae, m. poet; here refers to comic poets.
   comoedia, -ae, f. comedy.
8 Athenae, -arum, f. Athens.
   autumo, 1. to say.
9 quo = ut (in a purpose clause containing a comparative).
   graecus, -a, -um. Greek.
10 nusquam. nowhere.
   factum. Supply *esse*. "I will say that it took place (supplying *illud
     factum esse*) nowhere, except where it is said to have taken
     place."
11 graecisso, 1. to imitate the Greek, be in the Greek manner.
12 atticisso, 1. to imitate the Athenians of Attica, to be in the
     Athenian manner.
   uerum (verum). (conj.). but, but rather.
   sicilicissito, 1. to imitate the Sicilians, be in the Sicilian manner.
13 antelogium, -ii, n. (Latin *ante* + Greek *logos*). a prologue, preamble.
14 demetior, -iri, -mensus. to measure out.
15 modius, -ii, m. a measure of grain; a peck.
   trimodium, -ii, n. (*tres* + *modius*). a three-peck measure.
   horreum, -i, n. a storehouse, barn.
16 narro, 1. to tell, relate, narrate.
   benignitas, -atis, f. kindness, friendliness, favor.

What mood is established by the Prologus? How does he maintain a
light touch? How does he try to make the story seem real? How does
he bring the audience into the action? How does he create a dramatic
illusion and then break it?

7-12 Does Plautus expect the references to Athens and the Greek language
    to appeal to the audience for their intellectual literary snobbery or
    for their derision of matters Greek? Why? What does the use of the
    coined word *sicilicissitat* add to the effect?

MENAECHMI

The action of the play takes place in Epidamnus, the modern city of Dyracchium, on the west coast of Greece. To the spectators' left is the front of the house of the courtesan Erotium; to the right is the front of the house of Menaechmus I. Characters enter and exit through the doors of these houses or by way of the street that runs in front of them. The play opens with the entrance of the Prologus, who delivers the following speech.

PROLOGUE

PR. *gesturing extravagantly*

	DIALOGUE
Salūtem prīmum iam ā principiō propitiam	1
mihi atque uōbīs, spectātōrēs, nuntiō.	2
apportō uōbīs Plautum -- linguā, nōn manū:	3
quaesō ut benignīs accipiātis auribus.	4
Nunc argūmentum accipite atque animum aduortite:	5
quam poterō in uerba conferam paucissuma.	6
Atque hoc poētae faciunt in cōmoediīs:	7
omnīs rēs gestās esse Athēnīs autumant,	8
quō uōbīs illud graecum uideātur magis.	9
ego nusquam dīcam, nisi ubi factum dīcitur.	10
atque adeō hoc argūmentum graecissat: tamen	11
nōn atticissat, uērum sicilicissitat.	12
Huic argūmentō antelogium hoc fuit:	13
nunc argūmentum uōbīs dēmensum dabō,	14
nōn modiō neque trimodiō, uērum ipsō horreō:	15
tantum ad narrandum argūmentum adest benignitās.	16

17 Syracusae, -arum, f. pl. Syracuse.
   senex, senis, m. old man.
18 nascor, nasci, natus. to be born, be produced.
   geminus, -a, -um. twin.
19 forma simili. albative of description.
20 internosco, -ere, -noui, -notum. internosse = internouisse (internovisse).
      to distinguish between, tell apart.
   mamma, -ae, f. breast.
21 neque adeo. nor yet.
   pario, -ere, peperi, partum. to bring forth, bear.
23 quis = aliquis. *ali-* is dropped after *ne.*
   uostrum = vestrum. of you (pl.)
24 septuennis, -e. seven years old.
25 onero, 1. to burden, load.
   merx, -cis, f. wares, goods, merchandise.
26 inpono, -ere, -posui, -positum. to put in.
   geminus, -i, m. a twin.
27 Tarentum, -i, n. Tarentum (a Greek commercial city in south Italy).
   aueho (aveho), -ere, -uexi, -uectum. to carry off.
   secum = cum se.
   mercatus, -us, m. market.
29 ludus, -i, m. play, game; (in plural) public games, shows.
   quom = cum
   illuc. (adv.). to that place.
30 mortalis, -is, m. or f. a mortal, a man.
   ut. (adv.). as.
   conuenio (convenio), -ire, -ueni, -uentum. to come together.
31 aberro, 1. to wander away.
32 Epidamniensis, -is, m. or f. a man or woman of Epidamnum.
34 perdo, -ere, -didi, -ditum. to lose.
35 despondeo, -ere, -spondi, -sponsum. to promise to give something away;
      to pledge. animum despondere = to give up one's spirit, to despair.
   aegritudo, -inis, f. sickness.
36 emorior, -mori, -mortuos. to die. emortuost = emortuos est.
38 auos (avus), -i, m. grandfather.
   surripio, -ere, -rupui, -ruptum. to take or snatch away. Supply *esse*:
      perfect passive infinite in indirect statement after *rediit nuntius.*
40 immuto, 1. to change.
   geminus, -i, m. twin.
41 diligo, -ere, -lexi, -lectum. to value highly, love.
   surruptust = surruptus est.
42 indo, -ere, -didi, -ditum. to put on, give to.
   domist = domi est.

Mercātor quĭdam fuit Syrācŭsīs senex.   17

eī sunt nātī fīliī geminī duo,   18

ita formā similī puerī, ut māter sua   19

nōn internōsse posset quae mammam dabat,   20

neque adeō māter ipsa quae illōs pepererat.   21

aside, confidentially

Vt quidem ille dīxit mihi, quī puerōs uĭderat: 22

ego illōs nōn uĭdī, nē quis uostrum censeat.   23

postquam iam puerī septuennēs sunt, pater   24

onerāuit nāuem magnam multīs mercĭbus.   25

inpōnit geminum alterum in nāuem pater,   26

Tarentum āuexit sēcum ad mercātum simul: 27

illum relīquit alterum apud mātrem domī.   28

Tarentī lūdī forte erant, quom illūc uenit.   29

mortālēs multī, ut ad lūdōs, conuēnerant: 30

puer inter hominēs ibi aberrāuit ā patre.   31

Epidamniensis quĭdam ibi mercātor fuit: 32

is puerum tollit āuehitque Epidamnum eum.   33

pater eius autem postquam puerum perdidit,   34

animum despondit: eāque is aegritŭdine   35

paucīs diēbus post Tarentī ēmortuost.   36

postquam Syrācŭsās dē eā rē rediit nuntius   37

ad auom puerōrum, puerum surruptum alterum   38

patremque puerī Tarentī esse ēmortuom,   39

immutat nōmen auos huic geminō alterī.   40

ita illum dīlexit, quī surruptust, alterum: 41

illĭus nōmen indit illī quī domīst,   42

43 Menaechmo: agrees with the dative *illi* (42) rather than with *nomen*, as
we would expect from English usage.
44 ipsus = ipse.
eodemst = eodem est.
45 memini, -isse. (perfect with present meaning). to remember.
facilius. comparative adverb from *facilis*.
46 quia. (conj.). because.
clamor, -oris, m. shouting, clamor.
flagito, 1. to demand something, to dun someone for debt. flagitarier:
passive infinitive.
47 mox. (adv.). soon.
erro, 1. to wander, go astray, make a mistake.
praedico, 1. to proclaim, say, declare.
48 idemst = idem est.
ambo, -bae, -bo. (dat.: ambobus). both.
49 redeundumst mihi = redeundum est mihi. "I must return."
50 examussim. (adv.). (amussis, -is, f., a rule or level used by carpenters).
exactly, precisely, perfectly.
disputo, 1. to examine, treat of, discuss, explain.
51 quis = aliquis (after *si*). with *uestrum* (gen. pl.).
quid = aliquid.
Epidamnum. The accusative is used instead of the locative because of the
idea of motion to Epidamnus implied in the sentence.
52 audacter (-iter). (adv.). boldly.
imperato, dicito: future imperatives.
53 ita ut det, unde... "on condition that he give (money), whence" (or "by
means of which").
54 nisi qui...dederit. "unless (he is one) who shall have given (me)..."
argentum, -i, n. silver; money.
nugae, -arum, f. pl. jokes, nonsense. nugas agere: to be a fool.
56 uerum (verum). (conj.). but.
illuc. (adv.). to that place.
abeo, -ire, -ii, -itum. to go from, depart.
asto, -are, -stiti. to stand at or by; to stand.
57 dudum. (adv.). a short time ago, just now.
59 divitiae, -arum, f. pl. riches, wealth.
nihil. translate with the partitive genitive *liberorum*. "He had no
children except his wealth."
60 adopto, 1. to adopt.
surrupticius, -a, -um. stolen, kidnapped.
61 dotatus, -a, -um. provided with a dowry (*dos, -otis*, f.).
62 heres, -edis, m. or f. an heir, heiress.
quom = cum.
obeo, -ire, -ii, -itum. to go to or against; to meet; with *diem*, to meet
one's day, to die.
63 rus, ruris, n. the country. rus: "to the country" (no preposition needed).
pluit, pluit (pf.). it is raining.
64 ingredior, -di, -gressus. to go into, enter.
fluuius (fluvius), -ii, m. river.
rapidus, -a, -um. seizing; swift, rapid (from *rapio, -ere*).
haud. (adv.). not at all, by no means.
longule. (adv.). rather far. (*longulus* is a diminutive of *longus*).

Menaechmō, idem quod alterī nōmen fuit;   43

et ipsus eōdemst auos uocātus nōmine.   44

aside, confidentially

Proptereā illīus nōmen meminī facilius,   45

quia illum clāmōre uīdī flāgitārier.   46

nē mox errētis, iam nunc praedicō prius: 47

idemst ambōbus nōmen geminīs frātribus.   48

Nunc in Epidamnum pedibus redeundumst mihi,   49

ut hanc rem uōbīs examussim disputem.   50

sī quis quid uestrum Epidamnum cūrārī sibi   51

uelit, audacter imperātō et dīcitō,   52

sed ita ut det, unde cūrārī id possit sibi.   53

nam nisi quī argentum dederit, nūgās ēgerit: 54

quī dederit, magis maiōrēs nūgās ēgerit;   55

uērum illūc redeō, unde abiī, atque ūnō, astō in locō.   56

Epidamniēnsis ille, quem dūdum dīxeram,   57

geminum illum puerum quī surrupuit alterum--   58

eī līberōrum, nisi dīuitiae, nihil erat.   59

adoptat illum puerum surruptīcium   60

sibi fīlium eīque uxōrem dōtātam dedit,   61

eumque hērēdem fēcit, quom ipse obiit diem.   62

nam rūs ut ībat forte, ut multum pluerat,   63

ingressus fluuium rapidum ab urbe haud longulē--   64

65 *rapidus* modifies implied *fluvius* as subject of *subduxit*.
    raptor, -oris, m. one who seizes, a kidnapper. (dat. with verb of taking
        away).
    subduco, -ere, -xi, -ctum. to draw from under; to take away, carry off.
66 abstraho, -ere, -xi, -ctum. to drag or pull away.
    crux, -ucis, f. a tree or pole for execution by crucifixion; torture,
        trouble, misery, destruction. i (*or* abi) in malam crucem:
        "Go to the devil!" "Go and be hanged!" (maxumam = maximam).
67 illi. i.e. to Menaechmus I.
    divitiae, -arum, f. pl. riches, wealth.
    euenio (evenio), -ire, -ueni, -uentum. to come forth; (with dative) to come
        to, to befall.
68 illic. (adv.). in that place.
    habito, 1. to live.
69 habet = habitat.
70 hodie. (adv.). today.
71 quaerito, 1. to seek. quaeritatum: supine expressing purpose after a verb
        of motion.
    germanus, -i, m. brother.
    suom = suum.
72 fabula, -ae, f. story; play.
73 quando. (adv.). when.
74 familia, -ae, f. here: families or troops of actors.
    soleo, -ere, -itus. to be used or accustomed to.
    mutarier: passive infinitive. With this verb the passive has the same
        meaning as the active, only it is intransitive = "to change."
75 hic. (adv.). here.
    leno, -onis, m. pimp.
    senex, senis, m. old man.
76 pauper, -eris, m. a poor man.
    mendicus, -i, m. a beggar.
    parasitus, -i, m. a sponger, parasite.
    hariolus, -i, m. a soothsayer, prophet.

rapidus raptōrī puerī subdūxit pedēs   65

abstraxitque hominem in maxumam malam crucem.   66

illī dīuitiae ēuēnērunt maxumae.   67

pointing to ME.I's house

Is illīc habitat geminus surruptīcius.   68

Nunc ille geminus, quī Syrācusīs habet,   69

hodiē in Epidamnum uenit cum seruō suō   70

hunc quaeritātum geminum germānum suom.   71

pointing to the houses on the stage

Haec urbs Epidamnus est, dum haec agitur fābula: 72

quandō alia agētur, aliud fiet oppidum,   73

sīcut familiae quoque solent mutārier: 74

pointing to the stage buildings and miming each character-type
as he lists them

Modo hīc habitat lēnō, modo adulescens, modo senex,   75

pauper, mendīcus, rex, parasītus, hariolus.   76

                                                   Exit

77 iuuentus (iuventus), -utis, f. youth; young persons.
Peniculo. For the dative case, see note to line 43 above.
    peniculus, -i, m. diminutive of *penis, -is*, m. a tail,
    hence, a little tail; a brush (used for dusting).
78 ideo. (adv.). for this reason.
quia. (conj.). because.
mensa, -ae, f. table.
quando. (adv.). when.
edo, edere (*or* esse), edi, esum. to eat.
detergeo, -ere, -si, -sum. to wipe off.
79 catena, -ae, f. a chain.
uincio (vincio), -ire, uinxi, uinctum. to bind.
80 fugitios (fugitivus), -a, -om, fugitive.
81 nimis. (adv.). too.
stulte. (adv.). foolishly.
mea...sententia. "in my opinion."
83 lubido, -inis, f. desire. lubidost = lubido est.
nequiter. (adv.). badly.
84 catena, -ae, f. chain.
eximo, -ere, -emi, -emptum. to take out, remove.
aliqui, aliqua, aliquod. any, some.
85 compedio, -ire, ---, -itum. to fetter, shackle.
anus, -i, m. an iron ring (used to bind the feet of prisoners).
lima, -ae, f. a file.
praetero, -ere, -trivi. to rub off or wear down in front.
86 excutio, -ere, -cussi, -cussum. to shake out, drive out.
clauos (clavus), -i, m. nail.
nugae, -arum, f. pl. (see line 54). nugae sunt eae: "these (ways of
    restraining prisoners) are nonsense."
87 adseruo (adservo), 1. to preserve, guard.
recte. (adv.). rightly, properly.
aufugio, -ere, -fugi. to flee or run away.
88 esca, -ae, f. food.
potio, -onis, f. drink.
uincio (vincio), -ire, uinxi, uinctum. to bind.
decet. it is fitting, proper.
89 mensa, -ae, f. table.
plenus, -a, -um. full.
rostrum, -i, n. beak of a bird; snout, mouth of an animal.
deligo, 1. to tie or bind fast.
90 edo, edere (*or* esse), edi, esum. to eat. *edit* is here an old subjunctive form.
poto, 1. to drink.

77-109 What do you learn of Menaechmus I's character and personality from
Peniculus' speech?

79-97 What sustained simile does Peniculus use here? Does this mode of thinking
seem appropriate to a man without resources and responsibilities? What
kind of influence can he be expected to have on Menaechmus I?

ACT I

*Peniculus, Menaechmus I's parasite, enters along the street from
the spectators' right, coming from the forum or market place.*

PE.   *introducing himself to the audience*

Iuuentūs nōmen fēcit Pēniculō mihi   77

ideō quia mensam, quandō edō, dētergeō.   78

drawing himself up and pontificating

Hominēs captīuōs quī catēnīs uinciunt   79

et quī fugitiuīs seruīs indunt compedēs,   80

nimis stultē faciunt meā quidem sententiā.   81

nam hominī miserō sī ad malum accēdit malum, 82

maior lubīdōst fugere et facere nēquiter.   83

nam sē ex catēnīs eximunt aliquō modō.   84

tum compedītī ānum līmā praeterunt   85

aut lapide excutiunt clāuom. nūgae sunt eae.   86

quem tū adseruāre rectē, nē aufugiat, uolēs, 87

escā atque potiōne uincīrī decet: 88

apud mensam plēnam hominī rostrum dēligēs.   89

dum tū illī, quod edit et quod pōtet, praebeās 90

91 arbitratus, -us, m. judgment, choice, wish.
   ad fatim (*or* affatim). to satisfaction, abundantly, sufficiently.
   cottidie = cotidie.
92 edepol. (exclamation). by Pollux!
   tam etsi (*or* tametsi). although.
   capital, pl. capitalia, n. a crime punishable by death.
93 facile. (adv.). easily.
   adseruo (adservo), 1. to preserve, guard.
   uinclum (vinclum), -i, n. a rope, bond, fetter.
   uincio (vincio), -ire, uinxi, uinctum. to bind.
94 istaec = istae (with the demonstrative or emphasizing particle -*ce*, here
      shortened to -*c*).
   nimis. (adv.). too.
   lentus, -a, -um. pliant, flexible, tenacious.
   escarius, -a, -um. consisting of food (*esca*).
95 quam magis = quanto magis. the more.
   extendo, -ere, -di, -tum. to stretch, extend.
   tanto...artius. the more firmly. artius: comparative adverb.
      arte: closely, fast, firmly.
   adstringo, -ere, -inxi, -ictum. to draw close, bind, tighten.
96 quo. (adv.). whither. The reference is to Menaechmus, but Peniculus has
      Menaechmus' house, to which he is going, in mind.
97 iudico, 1. to judge, condemn; to adjudge, to put something or someone under
      someone else's power or authority (e.g., of debtors and creditors).
98 illic = ille. (for -c, see *istaec*, line 94).
   uerum (verum). (conj.). but, but rather.
   educo, 1. to bring up (a child), to rear; here, to fatten up.
99 recreo, 1. to make anew, to restore, revive, refresh.
   melius. (comparative adv., from *bene*). better.
   medicina, -ae, f. medicine, remedy, cure.
100 itast = ita est.
   ipsus = ipse.
   escae maxumae (= maximae). gen. of description. "(a man) of greatest
      food" = a glutton or a lavish entertainer.
101 Cerialis, -e. of, belonging to, or appropriate to Ceres, the goddess of
      agriculture (perhaps used here with a reference to the feasts at the
      festival of Ceres).
   cena, -ae, f. dinner, banquet, feast.
   mensa, -ae, f. table.
   exstruo, -ere, -xi, -ctum. to pile, heap up.
102 struix, -icis, f. a heap, pile.
   concinno, 1. to join together, order, arrange, prepare.
   patinarius, -a, -um. of dishes. (patina, -ae, f. a pan, dish).
103 standumst = standum est. it is necessary to stand.
   lectus, -i, m. bed, couch, dining-couch.
   quid = aliquid (after *si*).
   summum, -i, n. the top.
104 mi = mihi.
   interuallum (intervallum), -i, n. a space between, an interval of time.
105 domi. at home.
   domo, -are, -ui, -itum. to tame, break (of animals); to subdue, overcome,
      vanquish.
   carus, -a, -um. dear; costly, expensive (with a play here on both meanings:
      "loved ones," "dear ones").

suō arbitrātū usque ad fatim cottīdiē,   91

numquam edepol fugiet, tam etsī capital fēcerit: 92

facile adseruābis, dum eō uinclō uinciēs.   93

ita istaec nimis lenta uincla sunt escāria: 94

quam magis extendās, tantō adstringunt artius.   95

pointing to ME.I's house

Nam ego ad Menaechmum hunc eō, quō iam diū   96

sum iūdicātus: ultrō eō, ut mē uinciat.   97

nam illic homō hominēs nōn alit, uērum ēducat   98

recreatque: nullus melius medicīnam facit.   99

itast adulescens: ipsus escae maxumae   100

Ceriālīs cēnās dat: ita mensās exstruit,   101

tantās struīcēs concinnat patināriās: 102

standumst in lectō, sī quid dē summō petās.   103

Sed mī interuallum iam hōs diēs multōs fuit: 104

domī domītus sum usque cum cārīs meīs: 105

106 edo, edere (*or* esse), edi, esum. to eat.
    carissumum = carissimum. most dear (i.e., expensive).
107 cari, -orum, m. pl. loved ones.
    instruo, -ere, -xi, -ctum. to set in order, draw up in battle array; to
        furnish, provide, equip. instruontur = instruuntur.
108 eum = Menaechmum.
    inuiso (inviso), -ere, -si, -sum. to go to see or visit.
    ostium, -ii, n. door.
109 eccum = ecce + eum. ecce: (demonstrative adv.), see! behold! here!
    progredior, -i, -gressus. to come forth, come out.
    foras. (adv.). out through the doors (*foris, -is*, f. door), forth, out.
110 ni = nisi. unless.
    stultus, -a, -um. foolish.
    sies = sis (subjunctive of *sum*).
    indomitus, -a, -um. untamed; untamable; wild.
    impos, -otis. not master of, not possessed of, without power over + genitive.
111 odium, -ii, n. hatred. Note the double dative: "that which you see to be
        hateful (lit., for hatred) to your husband."
    tute = emphatic *tu*.
    habeas: "you would consider it (i.e. *quod viro esse odio uideas*) to be hate-
        ful to yourself."
112 praeterhac. (adv.). besides, furthermore.
    talis, -e. such. Here neuter sing. = "such a thing."
113 faxis = facias.
    faxo = faciam.
    foris. (adv.). out of doors, abroad.
    uiduos (viduus), -a, -om. widowed, divorced.
    uiso (viso), -ere, -si, -sum. to go to see, to visit.
114 quotiens. (adv.). as often as.
    foras. (adv.). out through the doors, forth, out.
    retineo, -ere, -ui, -tentum. to hold back, retain.
    reuoco (revoco), 1. to call back.
    rogito, 1. to ask eagerly or frequently.
116 egerim. perfect subjunctive: "what I did." This is what his wife would
        ask him when he returns rather than when he is leaving.
117 portitor, -oris, m. a toll-collector, custom-house officer (from *portus*,
        -us, m. harbor, port).
    domum. to home.
118 eloquor, -i, elocutus. to speak out, declare. eloquist = eloqui est.
    Word order: mihi necesse est omnem rem eloqui.
    quisquis, quaeque, quicquid. whoever, whatever.
119 nimium. (adv.). too much, too.
    delicatus, -a, -um. luxurious, indulged, spoiled.
    ut facturus (sim): i.e., "how I am about to act," "what I am about to do."
    Indirect question depending on *dicam*.
120 quando. (conj.). since.
    ancilla, -ae, f. a female slave.
    penus, -us, m. provisions, food.

110-181 Peniculus talks in terms of chains and fetters. By what bonds is Menaechmus I
       held? How is he freeing himself today?
110-122 What picture of the Roman wife's duties emerges?

nam neque edō neque emō, nisi quod est cārissumum.   106

id quoque: iam cārī, quī instruontur, dēserunt.   107

going up to ME.I's door

Nunc ad eum inuīsō.

*The door of ME.I's house opens, and ME.I appears wearing a
pallium or cloak, the usual Greek garment worn by men in Roman
comedies, but with a woman's palla or mantle concealed underneath it. PE. steps back from the door.*

                        Sed aperītur ostium: 108

Menaechmum eccum ipsum uideō: prōgreditur forās.   109

*ME.I enters, shouting angrily back at his wife (visible through
the open door), as he leaves the house. He does not see PE.*

SONG

ME.I Nī mala, nī stulta siēs, nī indomita imposque animī,   110

        quod uirō esse odiō uideās, tūte tibi odiō habeās.   111

        praeterhāc sī mihi tāle post hunc diem   112

        faxis, faxō forīs uidua uīsās patrem.   113

        nam quotiens forās īre uolō, mē retinēs, reuocās, rogitās,   114

        quō ego eam, quam rem agam, quid negōtī geram,   115

        quid petam, quid feram, quid forīs ēgerim.   116

        portitōrem domum dūxī: ita omnem mihi   117

        rem necesse ēloquīst, quicquid ēgī atque agō.   118

        nimium ego tē habuī dēlicātam.

                        pausing, then threateningly

                        Nunc adeō, ut factūrus, dīcam.   119

with increasing anger

Quandō ego tibi ancillās, penum,   120

120a lana, -ae, f. wool.
aurum, -i, n. gold.
purpura, -ae, f. purple; purple cloth; purple clothes.
121 egeo, -ere, -ui. to need, want, lack (here with acc.).
121a caueo (caveo), -ere, caui, cautum. to beware, watch out for + abl.
sapio, -ere, -ii. to be sensible, wise.
122 obseruo (observo), 1. to watch, observe.
desino, -ere, -sii. to cease, stop.
123 nequiquam. (adv.). in vain.
industria, -ae, f. diligence, activity, industry.
124 hodie. (adv.). today.
scortum, -i, n. a courtesan.
cena, -ae, f. dinner.
aliquo. (adv.). to some place, somewhere.
condico, -ere, -xi, -ctum. to talk over together, agree upon; engage
    oneself (for a meal with someone).
foras. (adv.). forth, out.
125 illic = ille.
simulo, 1. to pretend.
male loqui: to curse, threaten.
126 foris. (adv.). out of doors, abroad.
ceno, 1. to dine.
profecto. (adv.). actually.
haud. (adv.). not at all, by no means.
ulciscor, -i, ultus. to punish.
127 euax. (interjection). good!
iurgium, -i, n. quarrel, strife, railing.
hercle. (exclamation). by Hercules!
tandem. (adv.). finally.
abigo, -ere, -egi, -actus. to drive away.
ianua, -ae, f. door.
128 amator, -oris, m. lover.
maritus, -a, -um. married. amatores mariti = adulterers.
donum, -i, n. gift.
quid. why...?
cesso, 1. to cease from, stop; to be at rest, be inactive.
    "Why do they cease from..." = "Why don't they..."
129 confero, -ferre, -contuli, collatum. to bring together, confer upon.
congratulor, -ari, -atus. to congratulate.
quia. (conj.). because.
pugno, 1. to fight.
fortiter. (adv.). bravely.
130 intus. (adv.). inside, within.
uxori: dat. with verb of taking away.
surripio, -ere, -rupui, -ruptum. to take or snatch away.
scortum, -i, n. courtesan.
131 decet, -cuit. it is fitting, proper.
dari...uerba. dare uerba = to deceive, cheat + dat.
facete. (adv.). wittily.
catus, -a, -um. sharp, wise, sly, crafty.

128-136 What imagery does Menaechmus I use to describe his feat? What does this imagery
tell about his personality? Is this imagery significant for the audience?

lānam, aurum, uestem, purpuram   120a

bene praebeō nec quicquam egēs,   121

malō cauēbis, sī sapis: 121a

uirum obseruāre dēsinēs.   122

*ME.I's wife disappears into the house. ME.I continues in
a lower voice.*

Atque adeō, nē mē nēquīquam seruēs, ob eam industriam   123

hodiē dūcam scortum ad cēnam atque aliquō condīcam forās.   124

PE. *to audience*

Illic homō sē uxōrī simulat male loquī, loquitur mihi: 125

nam sī forīs cēnat, profectō mē, haud uxōrem, ulciscitur.   126

ΙE.I *to himself, still not noticing PE.*

Euax, iurgiō hercle tandem uxōrem abēgī ab iānuā.   127

ubi sunt amātōrēs marītī? dōna quid cessant mihi   128

conferre omnēs congrātulantēs, quia pugnāuī fortiter?   129

pulling aside his pallium *to reveal his wife's* palla *underneath*

Hanc modo uxōrī intus pallam surrupuī.

                                   pointing to ER.'s house

                              Ad scortum ferō.   130

sīc hoc decet, darī facētē uerba custōdī catae.   131

132 facinus, -oris, n. a deed, act.
pulcher, -chra, -chrum. beautiful. pulchrumst = pulchrum est.
lepidus, -a, -um. charming, elegant, neat, smart.
fabre. (adv.). skillfully, ingeniously, in a workmanlike manner
(faber, -bri, m. a workman, craftsman).
133 meo malo: ablative of manner without *cum*, "with evil to me," "to my loss."
aufero, auferre, abstuli, ablatum. to take away, steal.
damnum, -i, n. harm, injury, loss. ad damnum deferetur: by "loss"
(of money), Menaechmus means the *scortum*.
134 auorto (averto), -ere, -ti, -sum. to turn away from; to remove, steal.
hostibus: the reference is to his wife.
nostrum...socium: gen. pl. = nostrorum...sociorum.
salute: ablative of manner, "to the safety of" (cf. 133 *meo malo*).
135 heus. (interjection). Hey, there!
ecqui, ecqua, ecquod. (interrogative adj.). any. Modifies *pars*.
istac = ista (abl.). Modifies *praeda*.
insum, -esse, -fui. to be in.
136 deuenio (devenio), -ire, -ueni, -uentum. to go to, arrive at, reach, come into.
immo. (adv.). nay, on the contrary.
ne time: Plautus uses *ne* with the imperative to express a prohibition.
137 quis: Plautus uses *quis* as an interrogative adjective.
homost = homo est.
commoditas, -atis, f. convenience, advantage, benefit.
opportunitas, -atis, f. fitness, convenience, favorable opportunity.
138 salueo (salveo), -ere. to be well, be in good health. salue: greetings! hello!
Quid agis? "What are you doing?" or "How do you do?"
genius, -i, m. the protecting spirit or genius of a person.
139 per tempus: in time, on time.
mi = mihi.
aduenio (advenio), -ire, -ueni, -uentum. arrive.
140 soleo, -ere, -itus. to be used or accustomed to.
omnis = omnes (acc. pl.)
articulus, -i, m. joint (connecting parts of the body), knuckle; limb,
member; point of time, moment.
141 uin = visne? "Do you wish?"
facinus, -oris, n. deed.
luculentus, -a, -um. full of light (*lux*), bright, splendid, excellent.
inspicio, -ere, -spexi, -spectum. to look into or at, to inspect.
quis: interrogative adjective.
coquo, -ere, -xi, -ctum. to cook.
coquos (coquus), -i, m. cook. Peniculus, as a parasite, thinks only of food.
142 quid = aliquid.
titubo, 1. to stagger, totter, reel. si quid titubatum est: the intransi-
tive verb is here used impersonally in the passive: lit., "if anything
was staggered" = "if there was any staggering"; i.e., if the cook made
any slip (in preparing the feast which Peniculus imagines that
Menaechmus is talking about).
reliquiae, -arum, f. pl. leavings, remains (of the meal). Peniculus as a
gastronomic expert will be able to judge the skill of the cook even from
the mere scraps of food left after the feast.

hoc facinus pulchrumst, hoc probumst, hoc lepidumst, hoc

factumst fabrē: 132

meō malō ā malā abstulī hoc, ad damnum dēferētur.   133

āuortī praedam ab hostibus nostrum salūte socium.   134

PE. *suddenly approaching ME.I and addressing him*

RECITATIVE

Heus adulescens, ecqua in istāc pars inest praedā mihi?   135

ME.I *recoiling and covering the* palla

Periī, in insidiās dēuenī.

PE. *reassuring ME.I*

Immō in praesidium: nē timē.   136

ME.I Quis homōst?

    PE. Ego sum.

        ME.I *relieved*

Ō mea commoditās, ō mea opportūnitās,   137

saluē.

    PE. *taking ME.I by the hand*

        Saluē.

        ME.I Quid agis?

PE. Teneō dexterā genium meum.   138

ME.I Nōn potuistī magis per tempus mī aduenīre quam aduenīs.   139

PE. Ita ego soleō: commoditātis omnīs articulōs sciō.   140

ME.I Vīn tū facinus lūculentum inspicere?

PE. Quis id coxit coquos?   141

iam sciam, si quid titubātumst, ubi reliquiās uīderō.   142

143   dic: imperative of *dico*.
     mi = mihi.
     enumquam. (adv.). ever.
     tabula, -ae, f. writing-tablet; painted tablet, painting, picture.
     pictus, -a, -um. painted.
     paries, -etis, m. wall.
144   Catameitus, -i, m. a corrupted colloquial Latin transliteration of the Greek
        Ganymedes. Ganymede(s) was a beautiful Trojan youth carried off by Zeus
        (Jupiter) in the form of an eagle to be his cup-bearer in his palace in
        the heavens.
     Venus, -eris, f. Venus, goddess of love.
     Adoneus, -ei, m. = Adonis, -nis *or* -nidis, m. a Cypriot youth loved by
        Venus because of his extraordinary beauty. Menaechmus, wearing the
        palla that he has stolen from his wife, thinks he is as captivating
        as Ganymedes or Adonis.
145   pictura, -ae, f. picture.
     attineo, -ere, -tinui, -tentum. to hold to; to belong to; to concern,
        pertain to.
     age: "Come now!"
     aspicio, -ere, -spexi, -spectum. to look at.
146   ecquid. (adv.). perchance; in any way.
     adsimulo, 1. to imitate, simulate, make oneself like something else.
     similiter. (adv.). similarly. Menaechmus poses as a Ganymedes or an Adonis.
     istic = iste.
     ornatus, -us, m. adornment, clothing.
147   lepidus, -a, -um. charming, elegant, neat, smart. lepidissime: voc.
     essuri: fut. act. participle of *edo, -ere, edi, esum*, to eat.
148   hoc quod ego te iubeo: i.e., hominem lepidissimum esse me (147).
        Peniculus obeys and addresses Menaechmus as *homo lepidissime*.
149   ecquis, ecquid. any one; any thing.
     audeo, -ere, ausus. to have a mind to do something, to be prepared, to
        intend; to dare.
     de tuo: from your own (stock), on your own.
     istuc. (adv.). to that, to it.
     addo, -ere, -didi, -ditum. to add.
     hilarus, -a, -um. merry, cheerful, joyous. hilarissime: voc.
150   pergo, -ere, perrexi, perrectum. to go on, continue, proceed.
     porro. (adv.). forward, onward.
     hercle. by Hercules!
     gratia. (adv.). on account of, for the sake of + gen. Here *qua gratia* =
        cuius rei gratia: "for the sake of what thing," "why."
151   litigium, -i, n. dispute, quarrel, strife.
     tibist = tibi est.
     eo. abl. of cause: "for that reason," "therefore."
     mi = mihi.
     abs = ab.
     caueo (caveo), -ere, caui, cautum. to be on one's guard, to beware.
     cautius: comparative of *caute* "cautiously." cautus, -a, -um (from *caueo*):
        careful, cautious.

---

144   Would these mythological references mean anything to Plautus' audience?
     How could they have learned about these Greek mythological characters?

ME.I Dīc mī, ēnumquam tū uīdistī tabulam pictam in pariete, 143

ubi aquila Catameitum raperet aut ubi Venus Adōneum? 144

PE. Saepe, sed quid istae pictūrae ad mē attinent?

ME.I *exposing the
      palla again
      and posing*

Age mē aspice. 145

ecquid adsimulō similiter?

PE. Quī istic est ornātus tuos?· 146

ME.I Dīc hominem lepidissimum esse mē.

PE. *unimpressed and bored*

Vbi essurī sumus? 147

ME.I *sharply*

Dīc modo hoc quod ego tē iubeō.

PE. *obeying, without enthusiasm*

Dīcō: homō lepidissime. 148

ME.I Ecquid audēs dē tuō istuc addere?

PE. Atque hilarissime. 149

ME.I *eagerly*

Perge porrō.

PE. *exasperated*

Nōn pergō hercle, nisi sciō quā gratiā. 150

lītigium tibist cum uxōre: eō mī abs tē caueō cautius. 151

152-3 clam uxoremst (uxorem est): "(There is a place) secret from my wife."
    pulchre. beautifully. pulchre habeamus: a variation on the familiar
       phrase *bene habere* "to enjoy oneself."
    comburo, -ere, -ussi, -ustum. to burn up, consume.
154 age. "Come now!"
    sane. (adv.). soundly, healthily, well; indeed, truly, certainly.
    igitur. (adv.). therefore.
    quando. (conj.). since.
    mox. (adv.). soon.
    rogus, -i, m. funeral pyre.
155 umbilicus, -i, m. the navel; middle, center. umbilicumst = umbilicum est.
    dimidiatus, -a, -um. half.
    mortuos (mortuus), -a, -om. dead
156 morare = moraris, *from* moror.
    quom = cum.
    obloquor, -i, -locutus. to speak against; to interrupt. obloquere =
       obloqueris.
    ecfodio, -ere, -fodi, -fossum. to dig out, scratch out, tear out.
       ecfodito: future imperative.
    solum, -i, n. bottom; ground; sole of the foot or of a shoe. An exaggerated
       expression: "tear my eye out right through the sole of my foot."
157 uerbum (verbum), -i, n. word.
    faxo = fecero.
158 foris, -is, f. a door; in pl., the two leaves of a door.
159 audacter. (adv.). boldly.
    leoninus, -a, -um. belonging to a lion(ess).
    cauom (cavum), -i, m. cave.
160 eu. (Greek interjection). well! bravo! good!
    edepol. (exclamation). by Pollux!
    ne. (an emphasizing particle). surely, indeed.
    opinor, -ari, -atus. to suppose, believe, think.
    esses. "you would be."
    agitator, -oris, m. charioteer.
    probus, -a, -um. good, proper, excellent.
161 quidum. (qui = old ablative form). in what manner? how? how so?
    respecto, 1. to look around or back. Menaechmus keeps looking back toward
       his mouse just as a charioteer looks back to see how closely his
       competitors are following him in the race.
    identidem. (adv.). continually.
162 aio, ais, ait, aiunt. to say; to say yes, to affirm.
163 ecquid. (adv.). perchance.
    odor, -oris, m. smell, scent, odor.
    quid = aliquid.
    olfacio, -ere, -feci, -factum. to smell something.
164 coniectura, -ae, f. a guess, conjecture. i.e., to guess as to what the
       smell might be or from what it might have come. The rest of this
       line has been lost.

ME.I Clam uxōremst ubi pulchrē habeāmus, hunc combūrāmus diem. 152, 153

PE. *eagerly*

    Age sānē igitur, quandō aequom ōrās, quam mox incendō rogum?   154

    diēs quidem iam ad umbilīcumst dīmidiātus mortuos.   155

ME.I Tē morāre, mihi quom obloquere.

                  PE. Oculum ecfoditō per solum   156

    mihi, Menaechme, sī ullum uerbum faxō, nisi quod iusseris.   157

ME.I *leading PE. away from the door*

    Concēde hūc ā foribus.

        PE. *moving from the door*

           Fiat.

             ME.I *leading him further away*

                Etiam concēde hūc.

                      PE. *moving further*
                           from the door

                      Licet.   158

ME.I *leading him still further from the door and glancing fearfully back at it*

    Etiam nunc concēde audacter ab leōnīnō cauō.   159

PE. Eu edepol nē tū, ut ego opīnor, essēs agitātor probus.   160

ME.I Quīdum?

        PE. *playfully*

           Nē tē uxor sequātur, respectās identidem.   161

ME.I *changing the subject*

    Sed quid āis?

        PE. Egone? id enim quod tū uīs, id āiō atque id nego.   162

ME.I Ecquid tū dē odōre possīs, sī quid forte olfēceris,   163

    facere coniectūram tēcum?...   164

165 collegium, -ii, n. a board or college of officials (here probably of augurs). Peniculus means that he could make as good a guess about the smell as could the official soothsayers. The first part of the line has been lost.
166 agedum. (age + dum). "Come now!"
odoror, -ari, -atus. to smell something. odorare: imperative.
oleo, -ere, -lui. to emit a smell, to smell of something.
abstineo, -ere, -ui, -tentum. to keep off or away, to hold back.
167 summum...uestimentum. "the top part of the garment."
olfacto, 1. to smell something.
uestimentum (vestimentum), -i, n. a piece of clothing, a garment.
muliebris, -e. belonging to a woman.
168 istoc = isto. ex istoc loco: i.e., the lower part of the *palla*.
spurco, 1. to make filthy, befoul, defile.
nasum, -i, n. nose.
inlutibilis, -e. that cannot be washed out.
169 igitur. (adv.). therefore.
hinc. (adv.). from this place.
lepide. (adv.). delicately, daintily, smartly.
fastidio, -ire, -ii, -itum. to feel disgust, loathing, or nausea; to shrink back from something.
decet, -cuit. it is fitting, proper.
170 furtum, -i, n. theft.
scortum, -i, n. courtesan.
prandium, -ii, n. lunch.
171 fuant = sint. tibi sint = "May you have."
*edepol. (exclamation). by Pollux!
recte. correctly.
172 eloquor, -i, -elocutus. to speak out, declare, say. elocutu's = elocutus es.
surripio, -ere, -rupui, -ruptum. to take or snatch away.
173 defero, -ferre, -tuli, -latum. to bring away, to bring, deliver to.
meretrix, -icis, f. courtesan.
174 adparo, 1. to prepare.
prandium, -ii, n. lunch.
eu. (Greek interjection). well! bravo! good!
175 diurnus, -a, -um. of or belonging to the day.
stella, -ae, f. star.
crastinus, -a, -um. of or belonging to tomorrow.
poto, 1. to drink.
176 expedite. (adv.). without impediment; promptly, readily; to the point.
fabulor, -ari, -atus. to speak. fabulatu's = fabulatus es.
foris, -is, f. a door; in pl., the two leaves of a door.
ferio, -ire. to strike, beat, knock.

PE.   ...captum sit collḡium.   165

ME.I *thrusting the lower part of the* palla *under PE.'s nose*

      Agedum, odōrāre hanc quam ego habeō pallam: quid olet?

                                              PE. recoils

                                              Abstinēs?   166

PE.   Summum oportet olfactāre uestīmentum muliebre: 167

      nam ex istōc locō spurcātur nāsum odōre inlūtibilī.   168

ME.I *offering another part of the* palla

      Olfactā igitur hinc, Pēnicule.

                                  PE. draws back again

                                  Lepidē ut fastīdīs.

                                        PE.   Decet.   169

ME.I Quid igitur? quid olet? respondē.

                              PE.   Furtum, scortum, prandium. 170

ME.I Tibi fuant quaequomque mē uīs: ita edepol rectē omnia 171

      ēlocutu's. nam ab uxōre hanc pallam surrupuī meā.   172

      pointing to ER.'s house

      Nunc ad amīcam dēferētur hanc meretrīcem Erōtium: 173

      mihi, tibi atque illī iubebō iam adparārī prandium.

                                  PE. *gleefully*

                                              Eu.   174

ME.I Inde usque ad diurnam stellam crastinam pōtābimus.   175

PE.   Eu expedītē fābulātu's.

                        about to knock on ER.'s door

                        Iam forēs feriō?

                              ME.I Ferī.   176

177   passum = passuum. mille passuum = a mile.
      commoror, -ari, -atus. to stop, delay someone or something.
         commoratu's = commoratus es.
      cantharus, -i, m. (Greek word). a large pot-bellied drinking vessel,
         a tankard.
178   placide. (adv.). softly, gently, quietly.
      pulto, 1. to strike, knock.
      metuo, -ere, -ui, -utum. to fear, be afraid.
      foris, -is, f. door: in pl., the two leaves of a door.
      Samius, -a, -um. of Samos, an island off the coast of Asia Minor,
         famous for its clay and fragile pottery made from it.
      sient = sint.
179   All but one letter of this line is missing from the manuscripts.
180   obsecro, 1. to beg, implore.
    *hercle. (exclamation). by Hercules!
      eapse = ipsa. (= *ea* + *pse* as in *ipse*). eapse = Erotium.
      eccam = ecce eam. "Behold her!" "Here she is!"
      exeo, -ire, -ii, -itum. to go out, come out.
181   satin = satisne (-*ne* interrogative particle). satis: here "completely."
      occaeco, 1. to blind. occaecatust = occaecatus est.
      prae. (prep. with abl.). in comparison with, compared with.
      candor, -oris, m. splendor, beauty.
         180-181 "Do you see the sun, how it is completely (*satis*) blinded
         (darkened, obscured) compared with the splendor of this body
         (i.e., Erotium's)?"
182   mi. vocative of *meus*.
      salue. greetings!
      Quid ego? What (about) me?
      Extra numerum es mihi. "You don't count, as far as I'm concerned."
183   istuc = istud.
      adscriptiuos (adscriptivus), -a, -om. written in, enrolled;
         enrolled as a supernumerary soldier.
      soleo, -ere, -itus. to be used or accustomed to.
         183 "That same thing (= that same treatment) is accustomed to
         happen to other supernumeraries in the legion (i.e., in the army)."
         Peniculus feels just as ignored and out of the reckoning as super-
         numeraries in the army.
184   istic. (adv.). there; here.
      hodie. (adv.). today.
      adparo, 1. to prepare.
185   poto, 1. to drink.

182-225 To what class of society does Erotium belong? What is her economic
       status? Matrona is legally subject to her husband, but to whom is
       Erotium responsible?

appearing to change his mind, and restraining the eager PE.

Vel manē etiam.

        PE. *disappointed*

              Mille passum commorātu's cantharum.   177

ME.I Placidē pultā.

        PE. *about to knock*

              Metuis credō, nē forēs Samiae sient,   178

.... 179

ER. 's door begins to open.

ME.I *to PE.*

Manē, manē, obsecrō hercle: eapse eccam exit.

                      ER. comes out from her
                      house. ME.I continues,
                      rapturously, addressing PE.

                      Ōh, sōlem uidēs   180

satin ut occaecātust prae huius corporis candōribus?   181

ER. *to ME.I, fondly*

Anime mī, Menaechme, saluē.

        PE. Quid ego?

            ER. *disdainfully*

                Extrā numerum es mihi.   182

PE. *resignedly*

Idem istuc aliīs adscriptiuīs fierī ad legiōnem solet.   183

ME.I *to ER.*

Ego istīc mihi hodiē adparārī iussī apud tē --

            PE. *interrupting ME.I*

                Proelium: 184

hodiē id fiet: in eō uterque proeliō pōtābimus.   185

186   bellator, -oris, m. warrior, soldier.
      erit inuentus: fut. pf. "will have been found."
      cantharo: "whichever of us will have been found to be the better
         warrior with the tankard..."
187-188 adiudico, 1. to grant, award, adjudge something to someone.
      adiudicato: future imperative.
      sies = sis.
189   uoluptas (voluptas), -atis, f. pleasure, delight; (of persons, as a
        term of endearment) my joy.
      aspicio, -ere, -spexi, -spectum. to look at, behold.
      odi, odisse. (perfect used with present meaning). to hate.
190   nequeo, -ire, -ii, -itum. (nequis = 2nd person sing.). not to be
        able, to be unable.
      quin. but that. nequis quin: "you cannot but."
      induo, -ere, -ui, -utum. to put on (a piece of clothing; used in the
        passive with an active sense and the thing put on in the accusa-
        tive). "You cannot but have put on something of hers" = "Surely
        you have put on something of hers."
191   induuiae (induviae), -arum, f. pl. something put on; clothes.
      induuiae tuae: "something for you to put on."
      exuuiae (exuviae), -arum, f. pl. something taken off; (as a military
        term) spoils stripped from a fallen enemy.
      rosa, -ae, f. rose.
192   facile. (adv.). easily.
      quisquam qui impetrant. Erotium switches from singular to plural in
        thinking of the multiplicity of her lovers. "You easily win (with
        your gifts) so that you are better in my eyes ($mihi$) than anyone
        (of my other lovers) who win my favors."
193   meretrix, -icis, f. courtesan.
      tantisper. (adv.). so long. tantisper...dum: so long as.
      blandior, -iri, -itus. to flatter, be agreeable to, allure.
194-195 nasum, -i, n. nose.
      abripio, -ere, -pui, -eptum. to tear off or away. Supply *esse*.
      mordicus. (adv.). by biting, with bites (*mordeo, -ere*: to bite).
        "Biting" here is used comically of passionate kisses. "For if you
        loved (him), you should already have bitten his nose off with your
        kisses."
196   exuuiae (exuviae), -arum, f. pl. spoils.
      facere: here used in a religious sense -- to make an offering of some-
        thing, to sacrifice or consecrate it to a deity.
      uoueo (voveo), -ere, uoui, uotum. to vow, promise. Menaechmus "offers"
        the *palla* to Erotium as "spoils" (from his battle with his wife).
197   cedo. (an old imperative). here! give! "Give it to me!"
      obsecro, 1. to beg, implore.
      salto, 1. to dance.
198   sanus, -a, -um. sane.
199   exuo, -ere, -ui, -utum. to take off (clothes).
      igitur. (adv.). therefore; at least.
      nimius, -a,-um. too much, too great, excessive. nimio...
        periculo: "with very great danger."

to ER.

Vter ibi melior bellātor erit inuentus cantharō,   186

tua est legiō: adiūdicātō, cum utrō hanc noctem siēs.   187, 188

ME.I *to ER.*

Vt ego uxōrem, mea uoluptās, ubi tē aspiciō, ōdī male.   189

PE. *pointing to the* palla ME.I *is wearing*

Interim nequīs quīn eius aliquid indūtus siēs.   190

ER. *inspecting the* palla

Quid hoc est?

        ME.I *to ER.*

           Induuiae tuae atque uxōris exuuiae, rosa.   191

ER. Superās facile, ut superior sīs mihi quam quisquam quī impetrant. 192

PE. *aside, sarcastically*

Meretrix tantisper blandītur, dum illud quod rapiat uidet.   193

to ER.

Nam sī amābās, iam oportēbat nāsum abreptum mordicus.   194, 195

ME.I *taking off his* pallium *and handing it to* PE.

Sustine hoc, Pēnicule: exuuiās facere quās uōuī uolō.   196

PE. *taking* ME.I's pallium

Cedo, sed obsecrō hercle, saltā sīc cum pallā posteā.   197

ME.I ego saltābō? sānus hercle nōn es.

           PE. egone an tū magis?   198

sī nōn saltās, exue igitur.

        ME.I *taking off the* palla

           Nimiō ego hanc perīculō   199

200 surripio, -ere, -rupui, -ruptum. to take or snatch away.
     hodie. (adv.). today.
     meo...animo: "in my opinion."
     Hippolyta. The queen of the Amazons: Hercules was ordered to fetch
          her girdle (*subcingulum, -i,* n.), and he had to fight a dangerous
          battle with these warrior-women before subduing their queen and
          stripping her of her girdle.
201 haud. (adv.). not at all, by no menas. haud...umquam = numquam
          "never."
     aeque magno...periculo: "with equally great danger."
     aufero, auferre, abstuli, ablatum. to take or carry off, to steal.
202 quando. (conj.). since.
     uiuis = es. una uiuis: "you alone are."
     morigerus, -a, -um. (mos + gero). compliant with, obedient to + dat.
          meis morigera moribus: (lit.) "compliant with my character" =
          sympathetic, appealing to me.
203 decet, -uit. it is fitting, proper.
     animatus, -a, -um. animated, disposed, minded. with *hoc...animo* as
          ablative of manner.
     amator, -oris, m. lover.
     probus, -a, -um. good, proper, excellent.
          203: "Proper lovers ought to be animated with that spirit."
204 qui quidem: "at least those who..."
     mendicitas, -atis, f. poverty, beggary.
     propero, 1. to hasten. Subjunctive in relative clause of characteris-
          tic.
     detrudo, -ere, -si, -sum. to thrust, drive; to bring or reduce to.
205 mina, -ae, f. a Greek unit of weight or money equivalent to 100 Attic
          drachmas or Roman denarii.
     istanc = istam.
     anno: abl. of time when = "last year."
206 plane. (adv.). clearly.
     ut ratio redditur: "as the account is reckoned."
207 scin = scisne.
     accuro, 1. to take care of, to do with care.
208 prandium, -ii, n. lunch.
     accurarier. present passive infinitive.
209 scitamenta, -orum, n. pl. delicate food. (from *scitus, -a, -um,*
          beautiful, elegant, fine).
     forum, -i, n. the market place.
     obsono, 1. to buy (used of food or provisions). *obsonarier* is pre-
          sent passive infinitive.
210 glandionida, -ae, f. a delicate cut of meat. Word found only here; a
          comic patronymic formed from *glandium,* a delicate kernel or gland-
          ule in meat, which in turn is a diminutive of *glans, glandis,* f.
          acorn.
     suillus, -a, -um. of or belonging to swine (*sus, suis,* m. or f.);
          here, of fresh pork.
     laridum, -i, n. bacon.
     pernonida, -ae, f. (a comic patronymic formed from *perna, -ae,* f.
          ham). a bit of ham.
211 sincipitamentum, -i, n. (semi + caput). half-a-head; cheek of a hog.
     porcinus, -a, -um. of a hog.

surrupuī hodīe.

        PE. *dryly*

              Meō quidem animō ab Hippolytā subcingulum   200

Herculēs haud aequē magnō umquam abstulit perīculō.   201

ME.I *giving the* palla *to ER.*

    Cape tibi hanc, quandō ūna uīuis meīs mōrigera mōribus.   202

ER. *fondly*

    Hōc animō decet animātōs esse amātōrēs probōs.   203

PE. *sarcastically*

    Quī quidem ad mendicitātem properent sē dētrūdere.   204

ME.I *to ER.*

    Quattuor minīs ego ēmī istanc annō uxōrī meae.   205

PE. *dryly*

    Quattuor minae periērunt plānē, ut ratiō redditur.   206

ME.I *to ER.*

    Scīn quid uolō ego tē accūrāre?

                  ER. Sciō: cūrabō quae uolēs.   207

ME.I Iubē igitur tribus nōbīs apud tē prandium accūrārier,   208

atque aliquid scītāmentōrum dē forō obsōnārier.   209

making PE. drool

Glandionidam suillam, lāridum pernōnidam,   210

aut sincipitāmenta porcīna aut aliquid ad eum modum,   211

212 madidus, -a, -um. moist, wet, soaked; soft, boiled, well done.
mi = mihi.
adpono, -ere, -posui, -positum. to put or place near; (of dishes)
    to serve up, set before someone.
mensa, -ae, f. table.
miluinus, -a, -um. of or belonging to a kite (a rapacious bird of
    prey). With *miluinam* supply *famem* "hunger."
suggero, -ere, -gessi, -gestum. to bring under, put under; to furnish,
    supply, excite, produce. miluinam (famem) suggerant: "make me as
    hungry as a hawk."
213 actutum. (adv.). quickly, immediately.
prodeo, -ire, -ii, -itum. to go forth.
forum, -i, n. market place.
214 iam. (adv.). right away, directly.
hic. (adv.). here.
coquo, -ere, -xi, -ctum. to cook.
poto, 1. to drink.
215 quando. (conj.). when.
propero, 1. to hurry.
216 sequere. imperative.
uero (vero). (adv.). in truth, to be sure, surely.
217 *hodie. (adv.). today.
perdo, -ere, -didi, -ditum. to destroy; to lose.
mereo, -ere, -ui, -itum. to deserve, merit, be worthy of; to earn,
    obtain, get; to buy, purchase.
diuitiae (divitiae), -arum, f. pl. riches, wealth.
    217 (lit.) "I wouldn't buy the riches of the gods on condition of
    losing you today."
218 euoco (evoco), 1. to call out.
intus. (adv.). from within.
coquos (coquus), -i, m. cook.
actutum. (adv.). quickly, immediately.
foras. (adv.). out of doors, forth, out.
219 sportula, -ae, f. a little basket.
argentum, -i, n. silver; money.
eccos = ecce + eos. ecce: see! here!
tris = tres.
nummus, -i, m. a coin; a *sestertius*; (in Plautus) a Greek coin, two
    drachmae.
220 abi: imperative of *abeo, -ire, -ii, -itum. to go away.
obsonium, -ii, n. provisions, meat, fish, etc.
adfero, -ferre, attuli, allatum. to bring.
221 defio, defieri, to be lacking, be insufficient.
quoiusmodi. of what kind.
hic. (adv.). here.

madida quae mī adposita in mensam miluīnam suggerant.   212

snapping his fingers

Atque actūtum.

    ER. Licet ēcastor.

        ME.I Nōs prōdīmus ad forum: 213

iam hīc nōs erimus. dum coquētur, interim pōtābimus.   214

ER. Quandō uīs, uenī: parāta rēs erit.

        ME.I Properā modo.   215

to PE.

Sequere tū.

    PE. *obeying eagerly*

        Ego hercle uērō tē et seruabō et tē sequar   216

neque hodiē ut tē perdam, meream deōrum dīuitiās mihi.   217

PE. and ME.I exit to the spectators' right, toward the forum.

ER. *going to her door and calling to the servants inside.*

ēuocāte intus Cylindrum mihi coquom actūtum forās.   218

Cylindrus enters.

ER. *to CY.*

Sportulam cape atque argentum.

        giving him three coins

        Eccōs trīs nummōs habēs.   219

CY. Habeō.

    ER. Abī atque obsōnium adfer. tribus uidē quod sit satis   220

neque dēfiat neque supersit.

        CY. *curious*

        Quoiusmodī hīc hominēs erunt?   221

223 facile. (adv.). easily.
     fungor, fungi, functus. (usually with abl., here with acc.). to
         perform, discharge, do. lit., "easily performs the function
         of eight men."
224 eloquor, -i, -locutus. to speak out, declare, state.
     conuiua (conviva), -ae, f. dinner guest.
     ceterum, -i, n. the rest, object of *cura* (imperative).
225 coquo, -ere, -xi, -ctum. to cook.
     accumbo, -ere, -cubui, -cubitum. to recline at table. Here the
         supine expressing purpose.
     cito. (adv.). quickly, soon.

ER.   Ego et Menaechmus et parasītus eius.

                                        CY. Iam istī sunt decem.   222

nam parasītus octo hominum mūnus facile fungitur.   223

ER.   Ēlocūta sum conuīuās: cēterum cūra.

                                        CY. Licet.   224

cocta sunt: iubē īre accubitum.

                              *CY. departs to spectators'
                              right, toward the forum.*

              ER. *calling after him*

                   Redī citō.

                                   CY. *calling back over his shoulder*

                                        Iam ego hīc erō.   225

                                   ER. exits into her house.

226 uoluptas (voluptas), -atis, f. pleasure, delight.
    nauita (navita), -ae, f. sailor.
227 quom = cum.
    ex alto: "from the deep (sea)."
228 dolus, -i, m. guile, fraud, deceit, deception. non dicam dolo = "to
    tell the truth."
229 aduenio (advenio), -ire, -ueni, -uentum. to arrive.
230 quaeso, -ere, -ii. to ask, beg.
231 quasi. (adv.). as if. quasi mare: "as if (we were) the sea," "like
    the sea."
    circumeo, -ire, -ii, circuitum. to go around, travel around.
232 quaesitum: supine expressing purpose; "to seek."
    geminus, -a, -um. twin.
    germanus, -i, m. brother.
233 quid modi: partitive gen.; "what limit."
    futurumst = futurum est = erit.
234 sextust = sextus est.
    operam dare: to pay attention to something + dat.
235 Histri, -orum, m. pl. inhabitants of Istria, a coastal area of Italy
    north of modern Venice.
    Hispani, -orum, m. pl. Spaniards.
    Massilienses, -ium, m. pl. (-is: acc. pl.). inhabitants of Massilia
    (now Marseilles, the seaport in southern France).
    Hilurii, -orum, m. pl. inhabitants of Illyria or Illyricum (the ter-
    ritory bordering on the eastern shores of the Adriatic Sea.)
236 superus, -a, -um. upper, higher. mare superum: the upper, i.e., the
    Adriatic Sea.
    exoticus, -a, -um. (Greek word). foreign, beyond the shores.
    Graecia exotica = Magna Graecia.
237 ora, -ae, f. shore, coast.
    Italicus, -a, -um. of Italy.
    omnis (acc. pl.).
238 circumuehor (circumvehor), -i, -uectus. to ride or sail around.
    acus, -us, f. needle, pin.
    quaereres...inuenisses: subjunctives in a contrary to fact condition.
239 appareo, -ere, -ui, -itum. to appear, be visible. Here = "if it
    existed at all."
    iam diu. long since.
240 quaerito, 1. to seek.
    mortuos (mortuus), -a, -om. dead.
241 inuenissemus...uiueret: subjunctives in a contrary to fact condition.
242 istuc = istud. "that fact," i.e., that he is dead.
    quaero...qui faciat: "I am seeking (someone) who might make..."
243 emortuos (emortuus), -a, -om. dead.
244 operam...sumere: to take up an effort, make an effort.
    praeterea: i.e., after finding out that he is dead.

226-272 What kind of a man is Messenio? How do his attitudes toward Menaechmus
II differ from those of Peniculus toward Menaechmus I?

ACT II

*Menaechmus II and his slave, Messenio, enter from the spectators'
left, coming from the harbor, where they arrived a short time before. They are followed by slaves carrying baggage. Menaechmus
II is dressed to look exactly like Menaechmus I.*

DIALOGUE

ME.II Voluptās nullast nāuitīs, Messeniō,   226

maior meō animō, quam quom ex altō procul   227

terram conspiciunt.

                       MES. Maior, nōn dīcam dolō,   228

sī adueniens terram uideās, quae fuerit tua.   229

sed quaesō, quam ob rem nunc Epidamnum uēnimus?   230

an quāsī mare omnīs circumīmus insulās?   231

ME.II Frātrem quaesītum geminum germānum meum.   232

MES. *impatiently*

Nam quid modī futūrumst illum quaerere?   233

hic annus sextust, postquam eī reī operam damus.   234

Histrōs, Hispānōs, Massiliensīs, Hiluriōs,   235

mare superum omne Graeciamque exōticam   236

ōrāsque Italicās omnīs, quā adgreditur mare,   237

sumus circumuectī: sī acum, crēdō, quaererēs,   238

acum inuēnissēs, sī apparēret, iam diū.   239

hominem inter uiuōs quaeritāmus mortuom: 240

nam inuēnissēmus iam diū, sī uīueret.   241

ME.II Ergo istuc quaerō certum quī faciat mihi,   242

qui sēsē dīcat scīre eum esse ēmortuom: 243

operam praetereā numquam sūmam quaerere.   244

245 uerum (verum). (conj.) but.
     uiuos = nom. sing.
     exsequor, -i, -cutus. to follow after, pursue.
246 cor, cordis, n. heart.
     carus, -a, -um. dear (+ dat.). quam...carus: how dear.
247 scirpus, -i, m. bulrush.
     nodus, -i, m. knot. In scirpo nodum quaeris: a proverb used of
        searching for something that does not exist.
     quin...redimus: "Why don't we return home?"
     hinc. from here.
248 historia, -ae, f. a narrative of events or of travels.
249 dictum, -i, n. that which has been said; an order, command.
     facesso, -ere, -cessi, -itum. to do, perform, accomplish.
        Here a jussive subjunctive: "Do what you're ordered!"
     datum: that which you are given.
     edo, edere (*or* esse), edi, esum. to eat. edis: archaic form of sub-
        junctive. The subjunctive is jussive: "Eat what you're given!"
     caueo (caveo), -ere, caui, cautum. to be on one's guard, watch out
        for, beware of + dat.
     malo: trouble.
250 molestus, -a, -um. troublesome, annoying.
     ne sis: don't be.
     tuo...modo. in your manner, i.e., to suit you.
     hoc: this business, the search for the lost brother.
     em. (interjection). see!
251 illoc = illo.
     uerbum (verbum), -i, n. word; a saying, phrase, sentence. Here re-
        fers to Menaechmus' words in lines 249-250.
     seruom. acc. sing.
252 paucis: supply *uerbis*.
     plus, pluris; pl. plures, plura. more.
     plane. (adv.). plainly.
     proloquor, -i, -cutus. to speak out, say.
253 uerum (verum). (conj.). but.
     nequeo, -ire, -ii, -itum. to be unable.
     contineri. The passive infinitive is here used in a reflexive sense:
        "to hold myself back," "to restrain myself."
     quin. but that. quin loquar: "but that I might speak," (to restrain
        myself) "from speaking."
254 audin = audisne.
     quom = cum.
     inspicio, -ere, -spexi, -spectum. to look at.
     marsuppium, -ii, n. pouch, purse.
255 uiaticatus (viaticatus), -a, -um. furnished with travelling money
        (*uiaticum*).
     admodum. (adv.). very.
     aestiue (aestive). (adv.). in a summer-like manner (*aestas, -atis,*
        f. summer), scantily (little money would be needed to travel in
        the summer).
256 ne. (interjection). surely.
     opinor, -ari, -atus. to suppose, believe, think.
     reuorto (reverto). to return. reuorteris: future perfect active.

uerum aliter uiuos numquam dēsistam exsequī: 245

ego illum sciō quam cordī sit cārus meō. 246

MES. *impatiently*

In scirpō nōdum quaeris. quīn nōs hinc domum 247

redīmus, nisi sī historiam scriptūrī sumus? 248

ME.II *sharply reproving MES.*

Dictum facessās: datum edis: caueās malō. 249

molestus nē sīs, nōn tuō hoc fiet modō.

MES. *aside, annoyed*

Em, 250

illōc enim uerbō esse mē seruom sciō: 251

nōn potuit paucīs plūra plānē prōloquī. 252

uerum tamen nequeō continērī quīn loquar. 253

to ME.II

Audīn, Menaechme?

holding up and shaking the marsuppium

Quom inspiciō marsuppium, 254

uiāticātī hercle admodum aestīuē sumus. 255

nē tū hercle, opīnor, nisi domum reuorteris, 256

257 nil = nihil.
 geminus, -i, m. twin.
 gemo, -ere, -ui, -itum. to sigh, groan, wail.
258 itast = ita est.
259 uoluptarius (voluptarius), -ii, m. a person devoted to pleasure
 (*uolputas*, *-atis*, f.), a voluptuary.
 potator, -oris, m. drinker.
 maxumi = maximi: superlative of *magnus*.
260 sycophanta, -ae, m. (Greek word). informer, slanderer, deceiver,
 cheat, sycophant.
 palpator, -oris, m. a stroker (*palpo*, 1. to stroke, caress); a
 flatterer.
 plurumi = plurimi: superlative of *multi*.
261 habito, 1. to live.
 meretrix, -icis, f. courtesan.
262 nusquam. (adv.). nowhere.
 perhibeo, -ere, -ui, -itum. to hold out, present; to assert, say.
 blandus, -a, -um. flattering, fawning, enticing, alluring, seductive.
 Here comparative. Supply *esse*: "are said to be."
 gentium: partitive gen. with *nusquam*: "nowhere in the world."
263 inditumst = inditum est. indo, -ere, -didi, -ditum. to put upon,
 give to.
264 quia. (conj.). because.
 ferme. (adv.). almost.
 damnum, -i, n. hurt, harm, damage, loss.
 deuortor (devertor), -i, -uorsus. to turn aside, turn in; put up,
 lodge at a place.
265 istuc = istud.
 caueo (caveo), -ere, caui, cautum. to be on one's guard, watch out for.
 cedo. (archaic imperative). give!
 dum. merely emphasizes the previous word. "Just give me the purse."
 marsuppium, -ii, n. pouch, purse.
266 Quid eo uis? "What do you want to do with it?
 metuo, -ere, -ui, -utum. to fear, be afraid of (followed here by *ab*
 and *de* with abl.).
267 duis: archaic subjunctive of *do, dare*.
268 amator, -oris, m. lover.
269 iracundus, -a, -um. easily provoked to anger, irascible, irritable.
 perditus, -a, -um. hopeless, desperate, ruined, lost. animi
 perditi: genitive of description; "of incorrigible disposition."
270 id utrumque: "both of these things."
 argentum, -i, n. silver; money.
 cauero: future perfect. Its object is *id utrumque*, which is expanded
 in the next line.
271 ne...neue. lest...and lest.
 delinquo, -ere, -liqui, -lictum. to fail, be wanting; to do wrong.
 irascor, -i, iratus. to be angry at + dat.
272 lubens (libens), -entis. willing. From *lubet* (*libet*): it pleases,
 is agreeable. me lubente: abl. absolute.
273 obsono, 1. to buy food or provisions.
 ex mea sententia: "in accordance with my opinion or wishes."

258-264 How is this description of Epidamnus important for the development of
 the plot?

	ubi nīl habēbis, geminum dum quaerēs, gemēs.	257
	nam itast haec hominum nātiō: in Epidamniīs	258
	uoluptāriī atque pōtātōrēs maxumī;	259
	tum sȳcophantae et palpātōrēs plūrumī	260
	in urbe hāc habitant: tum meretrīcēs mulierēs	261
	nusquam perhibentur blandiōrēs gentium.	262
	proptereā huic urbī nōmen Epidamnō inditumst,	263
	quia nēmō fermē hūc sine damnō dēuortitur.	264
ME.II	Ego istuc cauēbō. cedo dum hūc mihi marsuppium.	265
MES.	Quid eō uīs?	
	ME.II Iam abs tē metuō dē uerbīs tuīs.	266
MES.	Quid metuis?	
	ME.II Nē mihi damnum in Epidamnō duis.	267
	tū magnus amātor mulierum es, Messeniō,	268
	ego autem homō īrācundus, animī perditī:	269
	id utrumque, argentum quandō habēbō, cāuerō,	270
	nē tū dēlinquās neue ego īrascar tibi.	271
MES.	*handing ME.II the* marsuppium	
	Cape atque seruā: mē lubente fēceris.	272

*CY. enters with his basket from the spectators' right, return-
ing from the forum where he had gone to buy provisions for the
prandium.*

CY.	*to himself*	
	Bene obsōnauī atque ex meā sententiā:	273

274 antepono, -ere, -posui, -positum. to set or place before.
   prandium, -ii, n. lunch.
   pransor, -oris, m. one who eats lunch; lunch-guests.
275 eccum = ecce + eum. ecce: (demonstrative adv.), see! behold! here!
   uae (vae). (interjection). an exclamation of pain or dread: "ah!"
       "alas!" "woe!" may be followed by dative.
276 prius...quam = priusquam. before. Translate with line 277.
   conuiua (conviva), -ae, m. or f. guest (for a meal).
   ambulo, 1. to walk.
   ostium, -ii, n. door.
277 obsonatus, -us, m. marketing.
   adeo, -ire, -ii, -itum. to approach.
   adloquor, -i, -locutus. to speak to, address.
278 salue (salve). greetings!
   di = dei.
   amo, 1. to love. Di te amabunt: a polite "Thank you!"
   quisquis, quaeque, quicquid. whoever, whatever.
282 certe. (adv.). certainly.
   insanust = insanus est. insanus, -a, -um. unsound in mind, mad,
       insane.
283 dixin = dixine.
   hic. (adv.). here.
   plurumi = plurimi: superlative of *multi*.
286 *eccum. = ecce + eum. ecce: (demonstrative adv.), see!
       behold! here!
   uidulus (vidulus), -i, m. suitcase, pack, knapsack.
   saluos (salvus), -a, -om. saved, unharmed; safe.

bonum antepōnam prandium pransōribus.   274

seeing ME.II

Sed eccum Menaechmum uideō. uae tergō meō: 275

prius iam conuīuae ambulant ante ostium,   276

quam ego obsōnātū redeō.

                    approaching ME.II

                    Adībō atque adloquar.   277

Menaechme, saluē.

              ME.II *surprised and puzzled*

                    Dī tē amābunt, quisquis es.   278

CY.   *puzzled in turn*

      Quisquis sum? nōn tū scīs, Menaechme, quis ego sim?   279

ME.II Nōn hercle uerō.

              CY.   *deciding that ME.II is joking*

                    Vbi conuīuae cēterī?   280

ME.II Quōs tū conuīuās quaeris?

                    CY. Parasītum tuom.   281

ME.II Meum parasītum?

              to MES.

              Certē hic insānust homō.   282

MES. *to ME.II*

      Dīxin tibi esse hic sȳcophantās plūrumōs?   283

ME.II *to CY.*

      Quem tū parasītum quaeris, adulescens, meum?   285

CY.   Pēniculum.

              MES. *patting his knapsack*

              Eccum in uidulō saluom ferō.   286

287 numero. (abl. used as adv.). lit., measured according to number or
        time; precisely, exactly, at the right time, on the instant;
        quickly, rapidly, soon; too quickly, too early.
     aduenio (advenio), -ire, -ueni, -uentum. to come, arrive.
     *prandium, -ii, n. lunch.
288 obsonatus, -us, m. marketing.
     hic. (adv.). here.
     pretium, -ii, n. money. quibus...pretiis: "for how much."
     porcus, -i, m. pig.
     ueneo (veneo), -ire, -ii, -itum. to go for sale, to be sold.
        Menaechmus has in mind buying a pig to be sacrificed in order to
        expiate Cylindrus' "insanity."
290 sacres: archaic plural of *sacer, sacra, sacrum.* dedicated or conse-
        crated to a divinity, holy, sacred. Here of sacrificial pigs.
     sincerus, -a, -um. clean, pure, sound.
     nummus, -i, m. the name of a Roman silver coin, also called a
        sestertius: (in Plautus) a Greek coin, two drachmae. nummis:
        supply *singulis.* singuli, -ae, -a: one to each, separate,
        single. nummis singulis: "for a *nummus* each," "two drachmas
        apiece."
291 pio, 1. to appease, propitiate by sacrifice; to purify with sacred
        rites.
292 equidem. (adv.). truly, indeed.
     *insanus, -a, -um. unsound in mind, mad, insane.
     certo. (adv.). certainly.
293 molestu's = molestus es. molestus, -a, -um. troublesome, annoying.
     ignotus, -a, -um. unknown.
     quisquis, quaeque, quicquid. whoever, whatever.
294 nosti = nouisti. pf. of *nosco*, to become acquainted with, pf. to know.
295 seu. or if.
     Coriendru's = Coriendrus es. There may be a play on the word
        coriandrum, coriander, an herb, the seeds of which are used for
        seasonings.
     perieris: perfect subjunctive used in a wish: "may you perish!"
297 tantum quod sciam: "as far as I know."
298 pro. (prep. with abl.). just as, as.
     *sanus, -a, -um. sound in mind, sane.
     *quom = cum.
299 ubi ego te nouerim: an indirect question dependent on an implied
        rogas.
300 era, -ae, f. the mistress of a house.

80ff What reason do all three, Menaechmus II, Cylindrus, and Messenio, give
      for their failure to understand one another? How does this reasoning
      contribute to the plot? Why does Menaechmus II not immediately suspect
      that the twin for whom he has searched for so many years lives nearby?

CY.   *ignoring MES.'s reply*

Menaechme, numerō hūc aduenīs ad prandium: 287

nunc obsōnatū redeō.

                    ME.II   *to CY.*

                        Respondē mihi,   288

adulescens: quibus hīc pretiīs porcī ūeneunt   289

sacrās sincērī?

                    CY. Nummīs.

                    ME.II *gesturing as if to hand*
                        CY. a coin

                        Nummum ā mē accipe: 290

iubē tē piārī dē meā pecuniā.   291

nam equidem insānum esse tē certō sciō,   292

quī mihi molestu's hominī ignōtō, quisquis es.   293

CY.   *baffled*

Cylindrus ego sum: nōn nostī nōmen meum?   294

ME.II   *annoyed*

Sī tū Cylindrus seu Coriendru's, perieris.   295

ego tē nōn nouī neque nouisse adeō uolō.   296

CY.   Est tibi Menaechmō nōmen.

                    ME.II   Tantum quod sciam.   297

prō sānō loqueris, quom mē appellās nōmine.   298

sed ubi nouistī mē?

                        CY. Vbi ego tē nouerim,   299

quī amīcam habēs eram meam hanc Erōtium?   300

ME.II Neque hercle ego habeō neque tē quis homō sīs, sciō.   301

303 cyathisso, 1. (Greek word). to ladle wine from the mixing-bowl to
          the drinking cup.
    *poto, 1. to drink.
    ei. (interjection). ei mihi: ah me! woe is me!
304 quom nihil est (mihi).
    qui = quo (abl. of means).
    dimminuo, -ere. to break into small pieces, to dash to pieces, to
          break.
305 tun = tune.
    soleo, -ere, -itus. to be used or accustomed to.
307 uero (vero). (adv.). truly.
    illisce = illis + demonstrative -ce.
    aedes, -is, f. house. The word frequently appears in the plural of a
          single house.
308 *habito, 1. to live.
    illi. (locative). there.
    perduint: archaic subjunctive of perdo, -ere, -didi, -ditum, to
          destroy.
309 insanio, -ire, -ii, -itum. to be insane.
    male dicere: to curse.
310 audin = audisne.
311 nummus, -i, m. the name of a Roman silver coin, also called a
          sestertius (see line 290).
    dudum. (adv.). just now.
    pollicitu's = pollicitus es. from polliceor, to promise.
312 certo. (adv.). certainly.
    sanu's = sanus es.
313 ipsus = ipse.
314 sapio, -ire, -ii. to be wise.
    porculus, -i, m. (diminutive). a little pig, a young pig.
    adfero, -ferre, attuli, allatum. to bring.

CY.   *bewildered*

Nōn scīs quis ego sim, quī tibi saepissimē   302

cyathissō apud nōs, quandō pōtās?

                              MES. *aside, angrily*

                                   Eī mihi,   303

quom nihil est, quī illī hominī dimminuam caput.   304

ME.II *to CY.*

Tūn cyathissāre mihi solēs, quī ante hunc diem   305

Epidamnum numquam uīdī neque uēnī?

                                   CY. Negās?   306

ME.II Negō hercle uērō.

                    CY. *pointing to ME.I's house*

                         Nōn tū in illīsce aedibus   307

habitās?

            ME.II *hotly*

                 Dī illōs hominēs, quī illī habitant, perduint.   308

CY.   *aside*

Insānit hic quidem, quī ipse male dīcit sibi.   309

to ME.II

audīn, Menaechme?

                    ME. Quid uīs?

                              CY. Sī mē consulās,   310

nummum illum quem mihi dūdum pollicitu's dare--   311

nam tū quidem hercle certō nōn sānu's satis,   312

Menaechme, quī nunc ipsus male dīcās tibi,   313

iubeās, sī sapiās, porculum adferrī tibi.   314

316 heu. (interjection). oh! ah! alas!
    hominem: acc. of exclamation.
    multus, -a, -um. much, (pl.) many; (here in a fairly rare sense) too
       much in evidence, tedious, wearisome, verbose, talkative.
    odiosus, -a, -um. hateful, odious.
317 *soleo, -ere, -itus. to be used or accustomed to.
    iocor, -ari, -atus. to jest, joke.
    illoc = illo.
318 quam uis: "as (much as) you wish," "very."
    ridiculus, -a, -um. funny, amusing.
319 aio, ais, ait, aiunt. to say; to say yes, to affirm.
    satin = satisne.
320 obsono, 1. to buy (used of food or provisions). obsonatumst =
      obsonatum est.
322 loquere = loqueris.
    urgeo, -ere, ursi. to press, impel, urge, burden, oppress.
    scelus, -eris, n. crime. Quod...scelus: "What crime besets you?"
      Messenio implies that feelings of guilt over some crime have
      driven Cylindrus insane.
323 qui = ut tu (introducing a result clause).
    molestus, -a, -um. troublesome, annoying.
    quid...rei: partitive genitive; "what thing." Quid tibi mecumst rei?
      "What is there with me with reference to you?" = "What do I have
      to do with you?" mecumst = mecum est.
324 fabulor, -ari, -atus. to speak, talk.
325 *certo. (adv.). certainly.

ME.II   *annoyed*

Heu hercle hominem multum et odiōsum mihi.   316

CY.   *aside, to the audience*

Solet iocārī saepe mēcum illōc modō.   317

quam uīs rīdiculus est, ubi uxor nōn adest.   318

to ME.II

Quid ais tū?

         ME.II   Quid uīs? inquam.

               CY.   *pointing to basket of provisions he*
                     is carrying

                       Satin hoc, quod uidēs,   319

tribus uobīs obsōnātumst, an obsōnō amplius,   320

tibi et parasītō et mulierī?

               ME.II   *puzzled*

                     Quās mulierēs,   321

quōs tū parasītōs loquere?

             MES.   *to CY.*

                 Quod tē urget scelus,   322

quī huic sīs molestus?

              CY.   *to MES.*

               Quid tibi mēcumst reī?   323

ego tē nōn nōuī.

        pointing to ME.II

          Cum hōc, quem nōuī, fābulor.   324

MES.   *to CY.*

Nōn edepol tū homō sānus es, certō sciō.   325

326 *ergo. (adv.). therefore.
    madeo, -ere, -ui. to be wet; to be drunk; to be softened by boiling,
        to be boiled, cooked.
    faxo = faciam. *faxo* is here parenthetical ("I'll see to it!") and not
        related to the main clause (*haec madebunt*).
    nil = nihil.
    moror, -ari, -atus. to delay. nil morabitur: "There'll be no delay."
327 proin = proinde. hence, therefore, accordingly.
    ne...abeas: subjunctive in a prohibition. abeo, -ire, -ii, -itum.
        to depart.
    quo = aliquo. anywhere.
    longius. (comparative adv.). very far.
    aedes, -is, f. (often in pl. with singular sense). house.
328 numquid. (adv.). numquid uis? "Do you want anything else?"
    ut eas: "that you might go..." "for you to go..."
    maxumam malam crucem: see line 66. *in* omitted here.
329 meliust = melius est. "it is better."
    accumbo, -ere, -cubui, -cubitum. to recline at table.
330 appono, -ere, -posui, -positum. to put or place at or on.
    Volcanus, -i, m. Vulcan, the god of fire, here = fire.
    uiolentia (violentia), -ae, f. violence.
331 intro. (adv.). inside.
    hic. (adv.). here.
    adsto, -are, -stiti. to stand at or near.
332 *hinc. (adv.). from here.
    abduco, -ere, -xi, -ctum. to lead or take away.
    potius quam. rather than.
    foris. (adv.). out of doors, outside.
333 abeo, -ire, -ii, -itum. to depart.
    haud. (adv.). not at all, by no means.
    mendacium, -ii, n. a lie, falsehood.
334 uerbum (verbum), -i, n. word.
    obseruo (observo), 1. to watch, watch out. obseruato: future imper-
        ative.
335 istic. (adv.). there.
    meretrix, -icis, f. courtesan.
336 ut + indicative. as.
    hinc. (adv.). from here.
337 qui. (archaic ablative form). how.
338 minime. (adv.). least of all; by no means, not at all, not in the
        least.
    mirus, -a, -um. wonderful, marvelous, astonishing, extraordinary.
        Supply *est*; "it's no wonder!"
339 seruolus (servulus), -i, m. (diminutive of *seruos*). a young slave.
    ancillula, -ae, f. (diminutive of *ancilla*). a young female slave.
340 si qua = si aliqua. aliqui, aliqua, aliquod. some, any.
    peregrinus, -a, -um. foreign.
    aduenio (advenio), -ire, -ueni, -uentum. to come, arrive.
341 rogito, 1. to ask.
    quoiatis, -is. (interrogative pronoun). whence? from what country?
    siet = sit.

CY.   *ignoring MES. and addressing ME.II*

    Iam ergō haec madēbunt faxō: nīl morābitur.   326

    proin tū nē quō abeās longius ab aedibus.   327

    about to go

    Numquid uīs?

        ME. *irately*

            Vt eās maxumam malam crucem.   328

CY. *angrily, then calming himself*

    Īre hercle meliust tē -- interim atque accumbere,   329

    dum ego haec appōnō ad Volcānī uiolentiam.   330

    ībō intrō et dīcam tē hīc adstāre Erōtiō,   331

    ut tē hinc abdūcat potius quam hīc adstēs forīs.   332

    CY. exits into ER.'s house.

ME.II Iamne abiit? abiit.

        to MES.

        Edepol haud mendācia   333

    tua uerba experior esse.

        MES. Obseruātō modo: 334

    nam istīc meretrīcem crēdō habitāre mulierem,   335

    ut quidem ille insānus dīxit, quī hinc abiit modo.   336

ME.II *puzzled*

    Sed mīror, quī ille nōuerit nōmen meum.   337

MES. Minimē hercle mīrum. mōrem hunc meretrīcēs habent: 338

    ad portum mittunt seruolōs, ancillulās: 339

    sī qua peregrīna nāuis in portum aduenit,   340

    rogitant quoiātis sit, quid eī nōmen siet: 341

342   postilla. (adv.). after that, afterwards.
      extemplo. (adv.). immediately, without delay.
      applico, 1. to join, fasten to. se applicare: to attach, apply,
         devote one's self to.
      agglutino, 1. to glue, fasten to.
343   pellicio, -ere, -lexi, -lectum. to allure, entice.
      perdo, -ere, -didi, -ditum. to ruin.
344   istoc = isto.
      praedatorius, -a, -um. plundering, rapacious. nauis praedatoria:
         pirate ship.
345   caueo (caveo), -ere, caui, cautum. to be on one's guard, to take care,
         take heed, beware.
      sane. (adv.). indeed, truly. "I think we must indeed beware of it
         (*abs qua*)."
346   recte. (adv.). correctly, rightly.
      demum. (adv.). indeed. tum demum: then indeed.
      sciam...caueris: future more vivid condition: "Then indeed I will
         know that I have warned you properly, if you take heed properly."
      caueris: fut. pf. ind.
348   taceo, -ere, -cui, -citum. to be quiet, be silent.
      dum. (as used here with imperative) a moment, a second, a little.
      parumper. (adv.). for a little while, for a moment.
      concrepo, -are, -pui, -pitum. to rattle, creak, sound, make a noise.
      ostium, -ii, n. door.
      egredior, -i, -gressus. come forth, come out.
350   asseruo (asservo), 1. to watch over, guard. asseruatote: future
         imperative (pl.).
      sultis = si uultis.
      naualis (navalis), -e. of or belonging to ships. nauales pedes: a
         comic circumlocution for "sailors."
351   sino, -ere, -sivi, situm. to let, allow, leave.
   *foris, -is, f. door; in pl., the two leaves of a door.
      sic. i.e., open.
      abeo, -ire, -ii, -itum. to go away, depart. abi: imperative.
      operio, -ire, -ui, -ertum. to shut, close. nolo (fores) operiri.
352   intus. (adv.). inside, within.
      opust = opus est. there is need.
353   sterno, -ere, stravi, stratum. (of a couch or bed) to spread, prepare,
         arrange, make.
      lectus, -i, m. couch, bed, dining-couch.
      odor, -oris, m. scent, odor, perfume, incense.
      munditia, -ae, f. cleanness, cleanliness, neatness, elegance.
354-355 inlecebra, -ae, f. an enticement, attraction, charm, bait, lure.
      amans, -antis, m. lover. animost = animo est.
356   amoenitas, -atis, f. pleasantness, delightfulness, loveliness.
         malost = malo est.
      lucrum, -i, n. gain, profit, advantage. lucro est: dative of purpose;
         "it is profitable, advantageous." Note the double datives in both
         clauses: "Loveliness is (for an) evil to the lover but profitable
         for us."

	postillā extemplō sē applicant, agglūtinant:	342
	sī pellexērunt, perditum āmittunt domum.	343
	motioning toward ER.'s house	
	Nunc in istōc portū stat nāuis praedātōria,	344
	abs quā cauendum nōbīs sānē censeō.	345
ME.II	Monēs quidem hercle rectē.	

MES. Tum dēmum sciam   346

rectē monuisse, sī tū rectē cāueris.   347

ER.'s door begins to open.

ME.II Tacē dum parumper: nam concrepuit ostium.   348

uideāmus, quī hinc ēgreditur.

MES. *setting down his knapsack*

Hoc pōnam interim.   349

to the other slaves, as he points to the baggage

Asseruātōte haec sultis, nāualēs pedēs.   350

ER. enters, addressing her slaves back through the door.

SONG

ER. Sine forēs sīc, abī; nōlo operīrī   351

intus parā, cūrā, uidē; quod opust fīat: 352

sternite lectōs, incendite odōrēs; munditia   353

inlecebra animōst amantium;   354, 355

amantī amoenitās malōst, nōbīs lucrōst.   356

357 illest = ille est.
coquos (coquus), -i, m. cook.
*aedes, -is, f. (often in pl. with singular sense). house.
aio, ais, ait, aiunt. to say.
eccum = ecce eum.
358 mi = mihi.
usui: dative of purpose in double dative construction: "who is useful
to me."
plurimum. (adv.). most, very much. (superlative of *multum*).
prosum, prodesse, profui. to be useful or of use, to benefit, profit.
359 hinc. (adv.). hence, for this reason.
potissimus, -a, -um. the chief, principal, most prominent, most
important (superlative of *potis*, -*e*; able, capable). "Likewise
hence it easily happens, as he deserves, that he is most important
in my house."
360 adeo, -ire, -ii, -itum. to approach.
adloquor, -i, -locutus. to speak to, address.
361 animulus, -i, m. (diminutive of *animus*, -*i*, m. mind, soul, heart).
used only in vocative as a term of endearment: "my heart," "my
darling."
mihi mira uidentur: plural where we would expect a singular: "it
seems strange to me that..."
362 hic. (adv.). here.
foris. (adv.). out of doors, outside.
quo = cui.
363 quom = cum. domus...haec: subject.
366 intus. (adv.). inside.
368 lubet (libet), lubuit, lubitum. (impersonal verb). it pleases, is
pleasing, is agreeable.
accumbo, -ere, -cubui, -cubitum. to recline at table. accubitum:
supine expressing purpose.
369 quicum = quocum (cum quo). with whom.
equidem. (adv.). truly, indeed, to be sure.
quid mecum tibi fuit: cf. 323.
370 negoti: partitive genitive dependent on *quid* (369).
quia. (conj.). because.
pol. (exclamation). by Pollux!

369ff. What kind of man does this scene reveal Menaechmus II to be?

looking around

Sed ubi illest, quem coquos ante aedīs esse ait?

seeing ME.II

                 Atque eccum videō,   357

quī mī est ūsuī et plūrimum prodest.   358

item hinc ultrō fit, ut meret, potissimus nostrae domī ut sit.   359

approaches ME.II

Nunc eum adībō: atque ultrō adloquar.   360

to ME.II

Animule mī, mihi mīra uidentur   361

tē hīc stāre forīs, forēs quoi pateant,   362

magis quam domus tua domus quom haec tua sit.   363

omne parātumst, ut iussistī   364

atque ut uoluistī, neque tibi   365

est ulla mora intus.   366

prandium, ut iussistī, hīc cūrātumst: 367

ubi lubet, īre licet accubitum.   368

ME.II *to MES.*

Quīcum haec mulier loquitur?

          ER. *to ME.II*

           Equidem tēcum.

            ME.II. *to ER.*

                          RECITATIVE

               Quid mēcum tibi   369

fuit umquam aut nunc est negōtī?

          ER. Quia pol tē ūnum ex omnibus   370

371   magnifico, 1. to make much of, to value greatly.

haud. (adv.). not at all, by no means. *haud* merely strengthens the negative expressed by *neque*.

immeritum, -i, n. to absence of guit or desert. immerito tuo: for no fault of yours. neque id haud immerito tuo: "and that not at all for no fault of yours" = "and richly deserved by you."

372   ecastor. (exclamation). by Castor!

benefacta, -orum, n. pl. benefits, benefactions.

floreo, -ere, -ui. to bloom, blossom, flower; to prosper, flourish.

373   ebrius, -a, -um. drunk.

374   ignotus, -a, -um. unknown.

compello, 1. to address, speak to. Here subjunctive in a relative clause of characteristic expressing result.

familiariter. (adv.). familiarly.

375   dixin = dixine.

istaec = istae.

hic. (adv.). here.

folium, -ii, n. a leaf.

376   praeut. (adv.). in comparison with, compared with.

triduom (triduum), -i, n. the space of three days, three days.

377 *meretrix, -icis, f. courtesan.

elecebra, -ae, f. (from *elicio, -ere, -licui, -licitum*. to draw out, entice, lure forth). a female allurer, enticer.

argentarius, -a, -um. of or pertaining to silver or money.

378   sino, -ere, sivi, situm. to allow, permit.

dum. merely emphasizes the imperative *sine* (cf. 265).

compello, 1. to address, speak to.

heus. (interjection). ho! ho there!

379   ibidem. (adv.). in the same place.

381   intro. (adv.). to the inside, within, in.

tetulit: a reduplicated form of *tulit*.

heia. (interjection). ah! come now!

deliciae, -arum, f. pl. delight, pleasure, charm; sport, frolic. delicias facere: to play tricks, to joke.

382   mi: vocative of *meus*.

quin: why...not? quin is: why don't you go?

amabo. lit., "I will love you"; colloquially = "please."

hic. (adv.). here.

rectius. (comparative of *recte*, straightly, uprightly, rightly, correctly, well). better.

384   nimis. (adv.). too much, very much.

negoti: partitive genitive dependent on *quid*.

oboleo, -ere, -ui. to smell of anything. Used with dative of reference of the person who smells something: *oboluit marsuppium huic* = "she smelled (your) purse."

385 istuc = istud.

Venus mē uoluit magnificāre: neque id haud immeritō tuō.   371

nam ēcastor sōlus benefactīs tuīs mē flōrentem facis.   372

ME.II   *to MES.*

Certō haec mulier aut insāna aut ēbriast, Messēniō,   373

quae hominem ignōtum compellet mē tam familiariter.   374

MES.   *to ME.II*

Dīxīn ego istaec hīc solēre fīerī? folia nunc cadunt,   375

praeut, sī trīduom hoc hīc erimus: tum arbōrēs in tē cadent.   376

nam ita sunt hīc meretrīcēs: omnēs ēlecebrae argentāriae.   377

sed sine mē dum hanc compellāre.

             to ER.

          Heus mulier, tibi dīcō.

                 ER. Quid est?   378

MES.   Vbi tū hunc hominem nōuistī?

              ER. Ibidem, ubi hic mē iam diū.   379

in Epidamnō.

        MES. in Epidamnō? quī hūc in hanc urbem pedem,   380

nisi hodiē, numquam intrō tetulit?

              ER. Heia, dēliciās facis.   381

to ME.II

Mī Menaechme, quīn, amābō, īs intrō? hīc tibi erit rectius.   382

ME.II   *to MES.*

Haec quidem edepol rectē appellat meō mē mulier nōmine.   383

nimis mīror, quid hoc sit negōtī.

            MES. *to ME.II*

               Oboluit marsuppium   384

huic istuc, quod habēs.

385   probe. (adv.). rightly, well, properly.
386   dum. see 378.
       scibo = sciam (fut. ind.).
       utrum...an. whether...or.
       mage = magis. more.
387   prandeo, -ere, -di, -sum. to eat lunch.
       tam = tamen.
       gratiast = gratia est. gratia: thanks. here = "no, thank you."
388   igitur. (adv.). therefore.
       coquo, -ere, -xi, -ctum. to cook.
       dudum. (adv.). a little while ago.
389   egon = egone.
390   quoi = cui.
       malum, -i, n. (a curse or term of abuse, usually in the vocative).
          plague, mischief, torment. sanast = sana est.
391   Peniculo: see on line 77. istest = iste est.
       qui = quo.
       extergeo, -ere, -si, -sum. to wipe off.
       baxea, -ae, f. a woven shoe worn on the comic stage and by philosophers.
392   scilicet. (adv.). certainly, naturally, obviously.
       dudum. (adv.). a little while ago.
393 *surripio, -ere, -rupui, -ruptum. to snatch or take away, to steal.
394   sanan = sanane.
395   cantherinus, -a, -um. of or pertaining to a horse, like a horse.
       ritus, -us, m. a religious rite; manner, way. cantherino ritu:
          in the manner of a horse.
       asto, -are, -stiti. to stand near or by, to stand.
       somnio, 1. to dream.
396   qui. why.
       lubet (libet), lubuit, lubitum. it pleases + dat.
       ludibrium, -ii, n. a laughing-stock, butt, jest, sport. dative of
          purpose: "why does it please (you) to consider me as a
          laughing-stock..."
       infitiae, -arum, f. pl. denial. idiom: infitias ire = to deny.
397   facta quae sunt: "what was done," "what you did."

ME.II. *to MES.*

       Atque edepol tū mē monuistī probē.   385

handing the marsuppium *to MES.*

Accipe dum hoc: iam scībō, utrum haec mē mage amet an marsuppium. 386

ER.   *to ME.II*

Eāmus intrō, ut prandeāmus.

       ME.II. *declining the invitation*

       Bene uocās: tam gratiast.   387

ER.   *puzzled*

Cūr igitur mē tibi iussistī coquere dūdum prandium?   388

ME.II   Egon tē iussī coquere?

       ER. Certō, tibi et parasītō tuō.   389

ME.II   Quoi, malum, parasītō?

       aside

       Certō haec mulier nōn sānast satis.   390

ER.   *answering ME.II's question*

Pēniculō.

       ME.II. Quis istest Pēniculus? quī extergentur baxeae?   391

ER.   Scīlicet quī dūdum tēcum uēnit, quom pallam mihi   392

dētulistī, quam ab uxōre tuā surrupuistī.

       ME.II. Quid est?   393

tibi pallam dedī, quam uxōrī meae surrupuī? sānan es?   394

to MES.

Certē haec mulier canthērīnō rītū astans somniat.   395

ER.   *to ME.II*

Quī lubet lūdibriō habēre mē atque īre infitiās mihi   396

facta quae sunt?

397   dic. **imperative.**

negem...fecerim. subjunctives in indirect questions, but note the
indicative *est*.

400   penetro, 1. to put or place something into something.

pedem penetrare: to enter.

401   prandeo, -ere, -di, -sum. to eat lunch.

egredior, -i, -gressus. to come forth.

conuenio (convenio), -ire, -ueni, -uentum. to come together, to meet.

eccere = ecce. lo! see! behold!

402   narro, 1. to tell, relate, report.

ligneus, -a, -um. made of wood.

403   tero, -ere, triui, tritum. to rub, grind, wear out. Here of a ship
whose hull has often been scraped.

fixam: from *figo*. "fixed," "fastened together," referring to the
planks of the hull being nailed to the ribs.

excutio, -ere, -cussi, -cussum. to shake or drive forth; to strike,
knock.

malleus, -i, m. hammer, mallet.

Menaechmus is describing a ship that has been frequently repaired.

404   quasi. (adv.). as if.

supellex, -lectilis, f. furniture. here of a furrier's rack with
many pegs in it.

pellio, -onis, m. a furrier.

palus, -i, m. a stake, prop. here of pegs on the furrier's rack,
which are compared to the pegs needed to secure the planks on
the aging ship.

proxumus (proximus), -a, -um. (superlative adj.). nearest, very
near + dat. proxumust = proxumus est.

405   amabo. please.

ludus, -i, m. play, game; joke, jest.

i. imperative of *eo, ire*.

hac. (adv.). this way, here.

406   nescio quem. some.

quaerito, 1. to seek.

407   prognatus, -a, -um. born from + abl.

408   perhibeo, -ere, -ui, -itum. to hold out, present; to say, assert; to
name. perhibere = perhiberis; 2nd person singular, passive:
"you who are said to have been born."

409-410   regnator, -oris, m. ruler.

iterum. (adv.). again, in turn.

411   tertium. (adv.). thirdly. Agathocles 317-289 B.C.; Hiero 265-215
B.C.; nothing further is known about the reigns of Phintia and
Liparo.

ME.II. *to ER.*

              Dīc quid est id quod negem, quod fēcerim? 397

ER.   Pallam tē hodiē mihi dedisse uxōris.

                      ME.II. *firmly*

                        Etiam nunc negō.   398

ego quidem neque umquam uxōrem habuī neque habeō, neque hūc   399

umquam, postquam nātus sum, intrā portam penetrāuī pedem.   400

prandī in nāuī, inde hūc sum ēgressus: tē conuēnī.

                    ER. *upset by the mention*
                           of the boat

                      Eccere,   401

periī misera, quam tū mihi nunc nāuem narrās?

                      ME.II. *jokingly*

                      Ligneam,   402

saepe trītam, saepe fīxam, saepe excussam malleō.   403

Quasi supellex pelliōnis, pālus palō proxumust.   404

ER.   *drawing ME.II toward her door*

Iam amābō, dēsiste lūdōs facere atque ī hāc mēcum simul.   405

ME.II Nesciō quem, mulier, alium hominem, nōn mē quaeritās.   406

ER.   Nōn ego tē nōuī, Menaechmum, Moschō prognātum patre,   407

quī Syrācusīs perhibēre nātus esse in Siciliā,   408

ubi rex Agathoclēs regnātor fuit, et iterum Phintia,   409, 410

tertium Liparō, quī in morte regnum Hierōnī trādidit,   411

412 Hierost = Hiero est.
  *haud. (adv.). not at all, by no means.
  falsus, -a, -um. false.
  praedico, 1. to proclaim, declare, say.
  pro. (interjection). O! Ah! By...
413 istaec = ista.
  illinc. (adv.). from that place, from there (i.e., from Syracuse).
  cate. (adv.). wisely, intelligently, clearly.
415 opinor, -ari, -atus. to believe, think; (here parenthetical) as I
      think, as I believe, in my opinion.
  pernego, 1. to deny altogether; to refuse, decline. Menaechmus means
      that Erotium's offer cannot be refused any longer.
  ne feceris: *ne* with the perfect subjunctive expresses prohibition.
416 periisti (from *pereo, -ire, -ii, -itum*, to perish). Perfect instead
      of future tense for vividness.
  intrassis = intraueris, fut. pf. of *intro*, 1. to enter.
  limen, -inis, n. threshold.
  quin...tace: "why don't you be quiet?"
417 adsentor, -ari, -atus. to assent, agree with + dat.
  quisquis, quaeque, quicquid. whoever, whatever.
418 hospitium, -ii, n. hospitality.
  iam dudum. just now.
420 inprudens, -entis. not foreseeing, unaware, ignorant, imprudent.
  aduorsor (adversor), -ari, -atus. to be against, to resist,
      oppose + dat.
  metuo, -ere, -ui, -utum. to fear, be afraid of.
421 renuntio, 1. to report, declare, announce.
422 quando. (conj.). since, because.
  intro. (adv.). within, in.
  etiam: "any longer."
423 floccus, -i, m. a piece of wool. as genitive of value in phrase
      flocci facere = to consider of trifling value, to take no
      account of.
424 intromitto, -ere, -misi, -missum. to send or let in.
  *ecastor. (exclamation). by Castor!
425 scin = scisne.
  amabo. cf. 382. here = "what I would like you to do."

425-430 Why does Erotium bring up the matter of alterations to the *palla*
      before they go in? (stage mechanics? characterization of Erotium?)

nunc Hierōst?

      ME.II *puzzled*

          Haud falsa, mulier, praedicās.

                MES. *to ME.II*

                   Prō Iuppiter,   412

num istaec mulier illinc uēnit, quae tē nōuit tam catē?   413

ME.II Hercle opīnor, pernegarī nōn potest.

                MES. *sternly*

                   Nē fēceris.   415

periistī, sī intrassis intrā līmen.

               ME.II Quīn tu tacē modo: 416

bene rēs geritur: adsentābor, quicquid dīcet, mulierī,   417

sī possum hospitium nanciscī.

               confidentially to ER.

               Iam dūdum, mulier, tibi   418

nōn inprūdens aduorsābar.

               pointing to MES.

               Hunc metuēbam, nē meae   420

uxōrī renuntiāret dē pallā et dē prandiō.   421

nunc, quandō uīs, eāmus intrō.

              ER. Etiam parasītum manēs?   422

ME.II Neque ego illum maneō neque floccī faciō, neque, sī uēnerit, 423

eum uolō intromittī.

           ER. Ecastor haud inuīta fēcerō.   424

caressing ME.II

Sed scīn quid tē amābō ut faciās?

           ME.II Imperā quid uīs modo.   425

426 dudum. (adv.). a short time ago, just now.
    phrygio, -onis, m. embroiderer (because the Phrygians were famous for
       their embroidery).
427 reconcinno, 1. to set right again, to repair, to rework.
    opera (plural of *opus*, *-eris*, n. work). here of decorations to be
       added to the *palla*.
428 qui. (exclamatory). how.
    recte. (adv.). rightly, correctly.
    eadem ignorabitur. "(although) the same, it will not be known (or
       recognized)."
430 *mox. (adv.). soon.
    aufero, auferre, abstuli, ablatum. to take away.
    auferto: future imperative.
    quando. (conj.). when.
    abeo, -ire, -ii, -itum. to go away, depart.
    maxime. (adv.). most of all, especially; certainly, by all means,
       yes.
431 *intro. (adv.). within, in.
    conloquor, -i, -locutus. to talk with + acc.
432 eho. (interjection). ho!
    quid negotist = quid negoti est? "What is it?"
    sussilio, -ire, -lui. (salio). to leap up, to jump. here imperative.
433 opust = opus est.
    scio ut me dices. "I know what you will call me."
    nequior. (comparative of *nequam*, indeclinable adjective: worthless,
       good for nothing, bad). Supply *es*: "(Then) you are so much
       (*tanto*) the worse."
434-435 praedam...operis. Meanechmus uses military language, as if he had been
      besieging Erotium's house. "I (almost) have the booty (i.e., the
      palla): I have begun such a great (thing of) work." opus, -eris,
      n. work (here of siege works deployed against a city).
    i. imperative of *eo, ire*.
    quantum potes. "as quickly as you can."
436 abduco, -ere, -duxi, -ductum. to lead away. abduc: imperative.
    taberna, -ae, f. shop; tavern; inn.
    actutum. (adv.). immediately.
    deuorsorius (deversorius), -a, -um. of or belonging to an inn or
       lodging-place. taberna deuorsoria: an inn.
437 facito: future imperative of *facio*. "See to it that (*ut*)."
    occido, -ere, -cidi, -casum. to fall down; to set. ante solem
      occasum: "before sunset."
    aduorsum (adversum). (adv.). against, toward.
    uenire aduorsum + dat. = to meet, to come and fetch.

ER.   Pallam illam quam dūdum dederās, ad phrygiōnem ut dēferās,   426

       ut reconcinnētur atque ut opera addantur quae uolō.   427

ME.II Hercle quī tū rectē dīcis: eadem ignōrābitur,   428

       nē uxor cognoscat tē habēre, sī in uiā conspexerit.   429

ER.   Ergō mox aufertō tēcum, quandō abībis.

                         ME.II *eagerly*

                               Maximē.   430

ER.   Eāmus intrō.

           ME.II Iam sequar tē: hunc uolō etiam conloquī.   431

    ER. exits into her house.

ME.II *to MES.*

    Eho, Messeniō, accēde hūc.

                 MES. *obeying*

                 Quid negōtīst?

                            ME.II Sussilī.   432

MES.   Quid eō opust?

          ME.II Opus est.

              MES. jumps as ordered

              ME.II Sciō ut mē dīcēs.

                   MES. Tantō nēquior.   433

ME.II Habeō praedam: tantum incēpī operis.

                   pointing to slaves with
                   the baggage

                 Ī, quantum potes,   434, 435

    abdūc istōs in tabernam actūtum dēuorsōriam.   436

    tū facitō ante sōlem occāsum ut ueniās aduorsum mihi.   437

438 erus, -i, m. master.
    fac tuom. fac: imperative of *facio*. "Mind your own business."
439 dolebit: impersonal use of the verb: "it will cause pain to" + dat. =
        "I will be sorry."
    quid = aliquid. anything.
    stulte. (adv.). foolishly, stupidly.
440 stultus, -a, -um. foolish, stupid.
    inscitus, -a, -um. ignorant, silly, stupid. inscitast = inscita est.
    quantum perspexi modo: "as far as I have seen just now."
441 abeo, -ire, -ii, -itum. to go away, depart.
    probe. (adv.). rightly, well, thoroughly, very, certainly.
442 lembus, -i, m. a kind of sailing vessel, a yacht.
    dierectus, -a, -um. crucified; here, by extension, of a "ruined" ship.
    praedatorius, -a, -um. of or belonging to pirates. nauis praedatoria:
        pirate ship.
443 inscitus, -a, -um. ignorant, silly, stupid.
    erus, -i, m. master.
    moderor, -ari, -atus. (moderarier: passive infinitive).
        to manage, rule, guide, direct + dat. "I who demand that I con-
        trol my master."
444 dictum, -i, n. saying, command. dicto...audientem: "obedient to his
        command."
    imperator, -oris, m. commander.
445 sequimini: imperative.
    imperatumst = imperatum est.
    ueniam aduorsum: see note to line 437.
    temperi. (adv.). on time.

MES.   *warning ME.II one last time*

Nōn tū istās meretrīcēs nōuistī, ere.

ME.II   *sharply*

Tacē, inquam et fac tuom:	438

mihi dolēbit, nōn tibi, sī quid ego stultē fēcerō.   439

mulier haec stulta atque inscītast: quantum perspexī modo,   440

est hic praeda nōbīs.

ME.II exits into ER.'s house

MES. Periī. iamne abīs? periit probē: 441

dūcit lembum dīerectum nāuis praedātōria.   442

sed ego inscītus quī erō meō mē postulem moderārier: 443

dictō mē ēmit audientem, haud imperātōrem sibi.   444

to slaves with baggage

Sequiminī, ut, quod imperātumst, ueniam aduorsum temperī.   445

MES. and slaves exit to spectators' left, toward the harbor.

446 plus. (adv.). more.
  triginta. thirty. "I have been born (i.e., alive) more than thirty
      years."
  interea loci: literally "meanwhile of place" (*loci*: partitive
      genitive) = simply "meanwhile."
447 quicquam: here used adjectivally: "any."
  facinus, -oris, n. deed, action.
  peior, -ius. (comparative of *malus*). worse.
  scelestus, -a, -um. wicked; unlucky, unfortunate.
448 contio, -onis, f. assembly.
  inmergo, -ere, -si, -sum. to dip, plunge, immerse.
449 hieto, -are. to open the mouth wide, gape, yawn.
  subterduco, -ere, -xi. to carry off secretly, to steal away.
      se subterduxit: he stole away. mihi: from me.
450 abeo, -ire, -ii, -itum. to go away, depart.
  amica, -ae, f. girl friend.
451 qui. (exclamatory). how.
  di = dei.
  perduint: archaic subjunctive of *perdo, -ere, -didi, -ditum*, to
      destroy. The subjunctive here expresses a wish.
  hoc: "this thing," i.e., *contionem habere* (452).
  comminiscor, -i, -mentus. to devise, invent.
452 qui: ablative: "by which."
  occupo, 1. to seize: to take up, occupy, employ. occupatus, -a, -um.
      busy.
453 otiosus, -a, -um. at leisure, unoccupied.
  decet, -uit. it is fitting, proper.
454 cito, 1. to summon.
  census, -us, m. the registering of Roman citizens; wealth, property;
      punishment imposed by a censor. censu capere: to be fined.
      "unless they are present when summoned, they should be fined."
  ilico. (adv.). immediately.
  Lines 455 and 456 have been lost from the manuscripts.
457 adfatimst = adfatim est. adfatim: enough + partitive genitive.
  in dies: "per day."
  esca, -ae, f. food; meal.
  edo, -ere, -edi, esum. to eat. edint: archaic subjunctive.
458 quibus negoti nihil est. (partitive genitive). "for whom there is
      nothing of business" = "those who have nothing to do."
  essum. supine of *edo, -ere* with two *s*'s instead of one. The supine
      expresses purpose: "to eat."
459 contio, -onis, f. assembly.
  dare operam: to pay attention to, attend to.
  comitia, -orum, n. pl. the assembly for electing magistrates.
460 perdo, -ere, -didi, -ditum. to destroy; to lose.
      esset...perdidissem: subjunctives in a contrary to fact condi-
      tion: "if it were thus,...I would not have lost."
461 quoi = cui. The antecedent is *ego* in the previous line. "I, to whom
      I believe that (he) wished (it, i.e., the *prandium*) to have been
      given as much as I see that I am living."

446-459 What responsive note do Peniculus' complaints awake in the audience?

ACT III

Peniculus enters from the spectators' right, coming from the forum.

PE.   *dejected*

Plūs trīgintā annīs nātus sum, quom intereā locī   446

numquam quicquam facinus fēcī pēius neque scelestius   447

quam hodiē, quom in contiōnem mediam mē inmersī miser: 448

ubi ego dum hietō, Menaechmus sē subterdūxit mihi   449

atque abit ad amīcam, crēdō, neque mē uoluit dūcere.   450

quī illum dī omnēs perduint, quī prīmus hoc commentus est,   451

contiōnem habēre, quī hominēs occupātōs occupat.   452

nōn ad eam rem ōtiōsōs hominēs decuit dēligī,   453

quī nisi adsint quom citentur, cēnsūs capiant īlicō?   454

.... 455, 456

adfatimst hominum, in diēs quī singulās escās edint,   457

quibus negōtī nihil est, quī essum neque uocantur neque uocant: 458

eōs oportet contiōnī dare operam atque comitiīs.   459

sī id ita esset, nōn ego hodiē perdidissem prandium: 460

quoi tam crēdō datum uoluisse quam mē uideō uīuere.   461

462 etiamnum = etiamnunc. even now.
    reliquiae, -arum, f. pl. the remains, the rest, the leavings, the
        scraps (of the meal).
    oblecto, 1. to delight, please.
463 corona, -ae, f. a wreath.
    exeo, -ire, -ii, -itum. to go or come out.
    *foras. (adv.). out of doors, forth.
464 subfero, subferre, sustuli, sublatum. to carry under; (here) to carry
        away, to clear away (the dinner). sublatumst = sublatum est.
    conuiuium (convivium), -ii, n. feast, banquet, dinner.
    aduorsum (adversum). (adv.). opposite to, against, toward. aduorsum
        uenire: to go or come to meet. uenio aduorsum: "I come to meet
        (him)."
    temperi. (adv.). on time.
465 obseruo (observo), 1. to watch.
    post. (adv.). afterwards.
    adeo, -ire, -ii, -itum. to go toward, approach.
    adloquor, -i, -locutus. to speak to, address.
466 potine = potisne est. "is it possible?"
    quiesco, -ere, -eui, -etum. to be quiet.
    probe. (adv.). rightly, well, properly.
467 lepide. (adv.). pleasantly, agreeably, finely, prettily.
    concinno, 1. to arrange properly, set right, repair.
    refero, referre, rettuli, relatum. to bring back.
    temperi. (adv.). on time.
468 faxo = faciam = a parenthetical "I'll see to it."
    eam = eadem "the same."
    ignorabitur: cf. 428.
469 phrygio: cf. 426.
    confecto prandio: abl. abs. "with the lunch finished."
470 uinum (vinum), -i, n. wine.
    expoto, 1. to drink up.
    excludo, -ere, -si, -sum. to shut out, exclude.
471 ni = nisi.
472 ultus...fuero = ultus ero. future perfect of *ulcisor, -i, ultus*. to
        take revenge for, avenge.
    obseruo (observo), 1. to watch.
473 pro. (interjection). O!
    di = dei.
    immortalis, -e. undying, immortal.
    quoi = cui.
474 boni...plus. "more of good," "more good."
    minor, minus. less.

466-523 What recurrent ideas are present in the scene between Menaechmus II and
    Peniculus? How do these themes add to the portrayal of the twins and
    to the development of the plot?
469 What is the importance of the *palla* as a symbol of Menaechmus I and his
    life, as a stage prop, and as a signal for prurient humor?

Ībō: etiamnum reliquiārum spēs animum oblectat meum.   462

Menaechmus II enters from Erotium's house, wearing a wreath
on his head and carrying the palla. *He does not see PE.,*
who continues speaking.

PE.   Sed quid ego uideō? Menaechmus cum corōnā exit forās.   463

sublātumst conuīuium.

                        sarcastically

                        Edepol ueniō aduorsum temperī.   464

withdrawing

Obseruābō, quid agat, hominem: post adībō atque adloquar.   465

ME.II   *speaking back through the door to ER. inside, and holding up*
        the palla.
                                                                         DIALOGUE
        Potine ut quiescās? ego tibi hanc hodiē probē   466

        lepidēque concinnātam referam temperī.   467

        nōn, faxō, eam esse dīcēs: ita ignorābitur.   468

PE.   *to himself, angrily*

        Pallam ad phrygiōnem fert confectō prandiō   469

        uīnōque expōtō, parasitō exclusō forās.   470

        nōn, hercle, is sum quī sum, nī hanc iniūriam   471

        mēque ultus pulchrē fuerō. obseruā quid dabō.   472

ME.II   *to himself, elated and holding up the* palla, *not seeing PE.*

        Prō dī immortālēs, quoi hominī umquam ūnō diē   473

        bonī dedistis plūs, quī minus spērāuerit?   474

475 prandeo, -ere, -di, -sum. to eat lunch.
poto, 1. to drink.
scortum, -i, n. prostitute.
accumbo, -ere, -cubui, -cubitum. to recline at table; (here) to lie
with, have intercourse with.
aufero, auferre, abstuli, ablatum. to take or carry off.
476 quoius = cuius.
heres, -edis, m. or f. heir, heiress. Menaechmus means that he will
make off with the *palla* so that no one will inherit it from
Erotium.
477 nequeo, -ire, -ii, -itum. to be unable.
exaudio, -ire, -iui, -itum. to hear clearly.
clanculum. (adv.). secretly, privately (i.e., from where he is
standing unobserved by Menaechmus).
478 satur, -ura, -urum. full (of food). parti: abl.
479-480 aio, ais, ait, aiunt. to say. Erotium is subject of *ait*.
me: subject of *dedisse* and *surrupuisse*.
481 *surripio, -ere, -rupui, -ruptum. to take away, steal.
482 erro, 1. to wander; to make a mistake, to be mistaken. Supply *eam*
(i.e., Erotium) as subject.
extemplo. (adv.). immediately
quasi. (adv.). as if, just as if. "as if I had business with her."
483 adsentor, -ari, -atus. to agree with.
quisquis, quaeque, quicquid. whoever, whatever.
484 uerbum (verbum), -i, n. word.
opust = opus est. "What need is there for..."
485 minor, minus. less.
nusquam. (adv.). nowhere.
bene fui: "I was well off."
dispensium, -ii, n. expense, cost.
486 adeo, -ire, -ii, -itum. to approach.
turbo, 1. to disturb, throw into disorder; to trouble.
gestio, -ire, -ii, -itum. to desire.
487 aduorsus (adversus). (adv.). opposite to, against. aduorsus ire: to
come to meet + dat.
ais: see 479-480
488 pluma, -ae, f. feather.
pessumus (pessimus), -a, -um. superlative of *malus*.
nequissimus, -a, -um. superlative of *nequam*, worthless, good for
nothing.
489 flagitium, -ii, n. a shameful or disgraceful act or thing; shame,
disgrace.
hominis: descriptive genitive with *flagitium*. "shame of a man" =
"shameful man."
subdolus, -a, -um. crafty, cunning, sly.
ac. ad.
minimus, -a, -um. superlative of *parvus*.
pretium, -ii, n. worth, value, price. minimi preti: genitive of
description: "(man) of smallest value."
490 qua...causa: "for which reason," "on account of which."
perdo, -ere, -didi, -ditum. to destroy, ruin.

	prandī, pōtāuī, scortum accubuī: abstulī	475
	hanc, quoius hērēs numquam erit post hunc diem.	476
PE.	*to himself*	
	Nequeō, quae loquitur, exaudīre clanculum:	477
	satur nunc loquitur dē mē et dē partī meā.	478
ME.II	*to himself*	
	Ait hanc dedisse mē sibi atque eam meae	479, 480
	uxōrī surrupuisse. quoniam sentiō	481
	errāre, extemplō, quasi rēs cum eā esset mihi,	482
	coepī adsentārī: mulier quicquid dīxerat,	483
	idem ego dīcēbam. quid multīs uerbīs opust?	484
	minōre nusquam bene fuī dispendiō.	485
PE.	*approaching ME.II*	
	Adībō ad hominem: nam turbāre gestiō.	486
ME.II	*to himself, as he sees PE. approaching*	
	Quis hic est, quī aduorsus it mihi?	

PE. *to ME.II, angrily*

	Quid ais, homō	487
leuior quam plūma, pessume et nēquissime,		488
flāgitium hominis, subdole ac minimī pretī?		489
quid dē tē meruī, quā mē causā perderēs?		490

491   ut: with indicative = "as," "when."
      dudum. (adv.). just now.
      forum, -i, n. market place.
492   funus, -eris, n. funeral, burial. fecisti funus...prandio (dat. of
        interest) "you buried (murdered?) the lunch."
      med = me.
      absens, -entis. absent. med absente: albative absolute.
493   ausu's = ausus es.
      quoi = cui. The antecedent is *prandio* (492).
      aeque. (adv.). equally.
      heres, -edis, m. or f. heir, heiress. Peniculus means that he should
        have had an equal share in the lunch.
494   quaeso, -ere, -ii. to seek; to ask. Here parenthetical: "I pray,"
        "I beg."
      rei: partitive genitive with *quid*. "What is there for you with me" =
        "What do you think you have to do with me?" mecumst = mecum est.
        cf. 369-370.
495   qui: antecedent of *tibi* (494). "you who."
      male dicere + dat. to speak ill of someone, to upbraid someone.
      ignotus, -a, -um. unknown.
      insciens, -entis. unknowing. "you who don't know me."
496   malam rem: trouble.
497   pol = edepol. by Pollux!
      eam: i.e., malam rem. Peniculus means that Menaechmus has already
        given him trouble by eating the lunch without him.
498   tibist = tibi est.
499   derideo, -ere, -si, -sum. to laugh at, scoff at, deride.
      quasi. (adv.). as if, just as if.
      noueris. Perfect subjunctive in clause of comparison. "as if you
        didn't know."
500   quod sciam. "as far as I know."
501   uerum (verum). (conj.). but yet.
      certo. (adv.). certainly.
      quisquis, quaeque, quicquid. whoever, whatever.
502   aequom facere: to act fairly, properly, reasonably.
      odiosus, -a, -um. hateful, troublesome, annoying.
      sies = sis (in a prohibition: negative *ne*).
503   uigilo (vigilo), 1. to be awake.
      equidem. (adv.). truly, indeed.
504   non negem, si nouerim: subjunctives in a future less vivid condition.
506   sanumst = sanum est.
      sinciput, -pitis, n. (from *semi-caput* "half a head"). brain; head.
507   surrupuistin = surrupuistine.
      uxori tuae: dative of separation after a verb of taking away.
508   istanc = istam.
510   satin = satisne.

	ut surrupuistī tē mihi dūdum dē forō,	491
	fēcistī fūnus mēd absente prandiō.	492
	cūr ausu's facere, quoi ego aequē hērēs eram?	493
ME.II	*baffled*	
	Adulescens, quaesō, quid tibi mēcumst reī,	494
	quī mihi male dīcās hominī hīc ignōtō insciens?	495
	an tibi malam rem uīs prō male dictīs darī?	496
PE.	Pol eam quidem edepol tē dedisse intellegō.	497
ME.II	Respondē, adulescens, quaesō, quid nōmen tibist?	498
PE.	Etiam dērīdēs, quasi nōmen nōn nōueris?	499
ME.II	Nōn edepol ego tē, quod sciam, umquam ante hunc diem	500
	uīdī neque nōuī: uērum certō, quisquis es,	501
	sī aequom faciās, mihi odiōsus nē siēs.	502
PE.	Menaechme, uigilā.	
	ME.II Vigilō hercle equidem, quod sciam.	503
PE.	*perplexed*	
	Nōn mē nōuistī?	
	ME.II Nōn negem, sī nōuerim.	504
PE.	Tuom parasītum nōn nōuistī?	
	ME.II Nōn tibi	505
	sānumst, adulescens, sinciput, ut intellegō.	506
PE.	Respondē: surrupuistīn uxorī tuae	507
	pallam istanc hodiē ac dedistī Erōtiō?	508
ME.II	Neque hercle ego uxōrem habeō, neque ego Erōtiō	509
	dedī nec pallam surrupuī. satin sānus es?	510

511 occisast haec res. occisast = occisa est. lit. "This affair has been
       slain," i.e., "it's ruined."
     induo, -ere, -ui, -utum. to put on (a piece of clothing; used in the
       passive with an active sense and the thing put on in the accusa-
       tive). "Didn't I see you wearing the *palla*?"
512 exeo, -ire, -ii, -itum. to go or come out.
     uae (vae). (interjection). woe! + dative.
513 cinaedus, -i, m. an effeminate man, a homosexual.
     quia's = quia es. quia: because.
514-515 tun = tune
     med = me.
     praedico, 1. to proclaim, say, declare.
516 uero (vero). (adv.). truly, indeed.
     abeo, -ire, -ii, -itum. to go away, depart. We would use a future:
       "Won't you go away?"
     quo dignus es: i.e., to the devil.
517 pio, 1. to appease, propitiate by sacrifice; to purify with sacred
       rites.
518 exoro, 1. to move, prevail upon, persuade by prayers.
519 uti = ut.
     eloquor, -i, -locutus. to speak out, declare, tell.
520 recido, -ere, reccidi, recasum. to fall back, to return.
     contumelia, -ae, f. abuse, insult, reproach.
521 faxo = faciam.
     inultus, -a, -um. unavenged, without paying the penalty.
     comedo, -ere, -edi, -esum. to eat entirely, to consume.
522 quid...negoti: partitive genitive. "What business is this?"
     satin = satisne. "Isn't it enough that..."
523 ludifico, 1. to make sport of, to make a fool of.
     concrepo, -are, -pui, -pitum. to make a noise.
     ostium, -ii, n. door.
524 *aio, ais, ait, aiunt. to say; to say yes, to affirm.
     multum. (adv.). much.
          amare ait te multum Erotium: "Erotium says that (she) loves you
          much" = "Erotium begs you."
525 ut...deferas: "to bring."
     una opera: "in the same manner," "at the same time"; i.e., along with
       the *palla*.

524ff What purpose is served by this short scene? Does it add anything to
        characterization or plot? Is it connected with a change of roles for
        the actors?

PE. *aside*

Occīsast haec rēs.

      to ME.II

      Nōn ego tē indūtum forās   511

exīre uīdī pallam?

      ME.II *incensed*

          Vae capitī tuō.   512

omnīs cinaedōs esse censēs, tū quia's?   513

tūn mēd indūtum fuisse pallam praedicās?   514, 515

PE. Ego hercle uērō.

      ME.II Nōn tū abīs, quō dignus es?   516

aut tē piārī iubē, homō insānissime.   517

PE. *threateningly*

Numquam edepol quisquam mē exōrābit, quīn tuae   518

uxōrī rem omnem iam, utī sit gesta, ēloquar.   519

omnēs in tē istaec recident contumēliae.   520

faxō haud inultus prandium comēderis.   521

PE. exits into house of ME.I.

ME.II *mystified*

Quid hoc est negotī? satin, ut quemque conspicor,   522

ita mē lūdificant?

      ER.'s door opens, and the ancilla *or slave*
      girl comes out holding a bracelet.

      sed concrepuit ostium.   523

AN. *to ME.II*

Menaechme, amāre ait tē multum Erōtium,   524

ut hoc ūnā operā sibi ad aurificem dēferās,   525

526   huc. (adv.). to this.
      addo, -ere, -didi, -ditum. to bring to, add to, join to.
      aurum, -i, n. gold.
      pondo. (adv.). by weight, in weight.
      uncia, -ae, f. (a measure of weight) the twelfth part of a pound,
         an ounce.
527   spinter, -eris, n. a bracelet.
      reconcinno, 1. to set right again, to repair. reconcinnarier:
         present passive infinitive.
528   istuc = istud.
      si quid = si aliquid.
529   dicito. future imperative.
      quisquis, quaeque, quicquid. whoever, whatever.
530   scin = scisne.
      nescio, -ire, -ii, -itum. not to know, to be ignorant.
      aureus, -a, -um. golden, made of gold.
531   olim. (adv.). once, once upon a time, formerly.
      clanculum. (adv.). secretly.
      armarium, -ii, n. a closet, chest (for storing money, food, or
         clothing).
532   uxori tuae: dative of separation with *surrupuisse*.
533   nunquam. (adv.). never.
      factumst = factum est.
      memini, -isse. (perfect system with present meaning). to remember.
      obsecro, 1. to beg, ask.
534   *igitur. (adv.). therefore.
535   immo. on the contrary.
      equidem. (adv.). truly, indeed.
      nempe. (conj.). indeed, certainly, to be sure.
536   istuc = istud. "the very one."
      armilla, -ae, f. a bracelet, armlet.
      una. (adv.). at the same time.
538   curare = te curaturum esse.
      dicito. future imperative
539-540   faxo = faciam. Supply *ut* with *referantur*.
541   amabo: "please."
      inauris, -ium, f. pl. (in + auris). ear-rings. inauris: acc. pl.
      da mihi faciendas: "have made for me."
542   pondo. (adv.). by weight, in weight.
      duom nummum: genitive plural dependent on *pondo*: "in the weight of
        two *nummi*," "two *nummi* in weight." nummus, -i, m. a Roman sil-
        ver coin, the *sestertius;* (in Plautus) a Greek coin, two drachmae.
        So here = "with the weight of four drachmae."
      stalagmium, -ii, n. (Greek word). an ear-drop, pendant.
543   libenter. (adv.). willingly, cheerfully, gladly.
      ueneris: perfect subjunctive

	atque hūc ut addās aurī pondō unciam	526
	iubeāsque spintēr nouom reconcinnārier.	527
ME.II	*to AN., as he takes the bracelet eagerly*	
	Et istuc et aliud, sī quid cūrārī uolet,	528
	mē cūratūrum dīcitō, quicquid uolet.	529
AN.	Scīn, quid hoc sit spintēr?	
	ME.II Nesciō, nisi aureum.	530
AN.	Hoc est, quod ōlim clanculum ex armāriō	531
	tē surrupuisse aiebās uxōrī tuae.	532
ME.II	Nunquam hercle factumst.	
	AN. Nōn meministī, obsecrō?	533
	redde igitur spintēr, sī nōn meministī.	
	ME.II *pretending to remember*	
	Manē.	534
	immō equidem meminī: nempe hoc est quod illī dedī	535
	istuc. Ubi illae armillae sunt, quas ūnā dedī?	536
AN.	Numquam dedistī.	
	ME.II Nam pol hoc ūnum dedī.	537
AN.	Dīcam cūrāre?	
	ME.II Dīcitō: cūrābitur.	538
	et palla et spintēr faxō referantur simul.	539, 540
AN.	*coaxingly*	
	Amābō, mī Menaechme, inaurīs dā mihi	541
	faciendās pondō duom nummum, stālagmia,	542
	caressing ME.II	
	ut tē libenter uideam, quom ad nōs ueneris.	543

544   fiat: "so be it."
      cedo. imperative: "give."
      aurum, -i, n. gold.
      manupretium, -ii, n. a workman's wages; pay for the work done.
545   sodes = si audes. audeo, -ere, ausus. to have a mind to do some-
         thing, to be prepared, to intend; to dare. sodes: "if you
         please."
      reddidero: future perfect in an emphatic assertion, instead of the
         simple future.
546   immo. on the contrary.
      cedo. imperative: "give."
      duplex, -icis. twofold, double.
547   quando. (adv.). when.
      dato. future imperative.
548   numquid. (interrogative adv.). numquid uis? "Do you want me any
         longer?" "Do you have anything further to say?"
      dicito. future imperative.
549   quantum possint: "as soon as possible."
      quique = qui + que. qui: ablative of price.
      liceo, -ere, -cui, -citum. to be for sale; to be valued at.
         qui liceant: "for whatever they are worth."
      ueneo, -ire, -ii, -itum. to go for sale, to be sold.
550   abeo, -ire, -ii, -itum. to go away, depart.
      operio, -ire, -ui, -ertum. to shut, close.
551   adiuuo (adiuvo), 1. to help.
552   cesso, 1. to delay, loiter, be inactive.
      mi = mihi.
553   lenonius, -a, -um. (leno, -onis, m. a pimp, pander, procurer).
      of or pertaining to pimping or pandering.
554   propero, 1. to hurry.
      profero, -ferre, -tuli, -latum. to bring forth, put forth.
      gradus, -us, m. step, pace.
555   demo, -ere, -mpsi, -mptum. to take off.
      abicio, -ere, -ieci, -iectum. to throw away.
      laeuus (laevus), -a, -um. left.
556   hac. (adv.). this way.
557   conuenio (convenio), -ire, -ueni, -uentum. to meet.

ME.II Fīat.

holding out his hand

    Cedo aurum; ego manupretium dabō. 544

AN. Dā sōdes abs tē; ego post reddiderō tibi. 545

ME.II Immō cedo abs tē: ego post tibi reddam duplex. 546

AN. Nōn habeō.

    ME.II At tū, quandō habēbis, tum datō. 547

AN. *about to go*

Numquid uīs?

    AN. exits into house of ER.

    ME.II *to AN. as she departs*

    Haec mē cūrātūrum dīcitō, 548

to himself

ut, quantum possint quīque liceant, uēneant. 549

looking at ER.'s door

Iamne abiit intrō? abiit, operuit forīs. 550

jubilant

Dī mē quidem omnēs adiuuant, augent, amant. 551

sed quid ego cessō, dum datur mī occāsiō 552

tempusque, abīre ab hīs locīs lēnōniīs? 553

properā, Menaechme: fer pedem, profer gradum. 554

taking off the wreath and throwing it away to spectators' right

Dēmam hanc corōnam atque abiciam ad laeuam manum, 555

ut, sī sequantur mē, hāc abiise censeant. 556

ībō et conueniam seruom, sī poterō, meum, 557

ut haec quae bona dant dī mihi, ex mē sciat. 558

*ME.II exits to spectators' left, toward the harbor where MES.
had gone with the slaves and baggage.*

559 frustra. (adv.). in deception, in error. frustra haberi:
      to be deceived, cheated. Supply *haberi*.
  matrimonium, -ii, n. marriage.
560 compilo, 1. to plunder, pillage, rob.
  clanculum. (adv.). secretly.
  *quisquis, quaeque, quicquid. whoever, whatever.
  domist = domi est. "is at home."
561 taceo, -ere, -cui, -citum. to be silent.
562 manufesto. (adv.). clearly, openly, evidently, manifestly.
  faxo = faciam. Here used parenthetically: "I'll see to it!"
  opprimes: supply *eum*. opprimo, -ere, -essi, -essum. to press
      against; to overwhelm, overcome; to fall upon, surprise, catch.
  sequere: imperative.
  hac. (adv.). this way.
563 phrygio, -onis, m. embroiderer.
  corona, -ae, f. wreath.
  ebrius, -a, -um. drunk.
565 *eccam = ecce eam. here it is.
  mentior, -iri, -itus. to lie.
566 em. (interjection). indeed! well! hah!
  *abeo, -ire, -ii, -itum. to go away, depart.
  persequor, -i, -cutus. to follow, pursue.
  uestigium (vestigium), -ii, n. footstep, track.
567 optume (optime). (superlative adv.). conveniently.
  reuortor (revertor), -i, -uorsus. to return.
569 male habeas: "treat him badly," "scold him."
570 aucupo, 1. (auis + capio). to go bird-catching; to lie in wait for,
      to watch for.
571 ut. (exclamatory). how.
  maxime. (adv.). especially.
  morus, -a, -um. foolish, silly. "how we make use of this espe-
      cially silly custom..."

559ff. Is the Matrona consistent with one's impression of her gained through
      Menaechmus I's remarks and attitudes?
571-595 Menaechmus I's experience as described in his song is a completely
      Roman one. Does it seem out of place in the Greek context? What
      effect could it be expected to have on the Roman audience? What does
      his experience add to our concept of his status and character? Can
      the song be understood as a satirical attack on Roman values and
      standards, as a "message" on the part of the playwright?

ACT IV

The matrona, *wife of Menaechmus I, enters from her house on the*
spectators' right, followed by PE., who has just told her what
her husband has been doing.

MA.   *angrily and tearfully*

Egone hīc mē patiar frustrā in mātrimōniō,   559

ubi uir compīlet clanculum, quicquid domīst,   560

atque ea ad amīcam dēferat?

                      PE. Quīn tū tacēs?   561

manufestō faxō iam opprimēs.

                leading MA. to the right, in
                the direction of the forum

                Sequere hāc modo.   562

pallam ad phrygiōnem cum corōnā ēbrius   563

ferēbat, hodiē tibi quam surrupuit domō.   564

catching sight of the wreath and picking it up

Sed eccam corōnam, quam habuit: num mentior?   565

looking toward the spectators' right

Em hāc abiit, sī uīs persequī uestīgiīs.   566

ME. I enters from the spectators' right, returning from the
forum. He does not see PE. and MA. PE. continues speaking.

PE.   Atque edepol eccum optumē reuortitur.   567

sed pallam nōn fert.

            MA. Quid ego nunc cum illōc agam?   568

PE.   Idem quod semper: male habeās: sīc censeō.   569

drawing her back and to the side out of sight of ME.I

Hūc concēdāmus: ex insidiīs aucupā.   570

ME.I   *in a bad temper*

                                      SONG

Vt hōc utimur maximē mōre morō   571

572 molestus, -a, -um. troublesome, irksome, annoying.
    multum. (adv.). very.
    uti. (exclamatory). how.
    quique sunt optumi: "whoever are the best people" = "all the best
        people." optumi = optimi.
573 maxume = maxime.
575 -ne an. whether...or.
    quaerito, 1. to seek, ask.
    res: (here) property, possessions, money.
577 quoiusmodi. of what kind or nature.
    clueo, -ere. to be named, called, spoken of. Menaechmus means that
        patrons are more concerned with the wealth of their clients than
        with their reputation for trustworthiness.
578 pauper, -peris. poor.
    nequam. worthless.
    habetur: "he is considered."
579 sin. but if.
    diues, -itis. rich.
    malust = malus est.
    frugi. (noun in dative case used as an indeclinable adjective). fit
        for food; useful, fit, proper, worthy.
580 aequom bonum: "that which is fair and good."
    usquam. (adv.). ever.
    colo, -ere, colui, cultum. to cultivate, practice, devote one's self
        to.
581 sollicitus, -a, -um. disturbed, anxious, troubled.
    patronus, -i, m. patron.
582 denego, 1. to deny.
    lis, litis, f. quarrel; lawsuit.
    plenus, -a, -um. full of + gen.
    rapax, -acis. grasping, greedy, rapacious.
583 fraudulentus, -a, -um. cheating, deceitful, fraudulent.
584 faenus, -oris, n. interest (from capital loaned out).
    periurium, -ii, n. a false oath, perjury.
    habent rem paratam: "have made their money."
584a querela, -ae, f. complaint, accusation.
585 dicitur dies: "the day for their trial is set."
586 quippe. (conjunction). for, since.
    qui: "they," i.e., the *patroni*.
    pro illis: "on behalf of those things."
    loquantur: subjunctive in relative causal clause.
    quae male fecerint: "which they (i.e., their clients) have done
        wrong." fecerint: perfect subjunctive.
587 ad populum: before the people assembled in the *comitia centuriata*.
    in iure: at law, before a magistrate.
    ad iudicem: before a judge (*iudex, -icis*, m.).
    rest = res est. res (here) = lawsuit. "Whether the lawsuit is tried
        before the people or..."
588 nimis. (adv.). too much, excessively, exceedingly.
    sollicitus, -a, -um. disturbed, anxious, troubled.

molestōque multum, atque utī quīque sunt op-   572

tumī, maxumē mōrem habent hunc: 573

clientēs sibi omnēs uolunt esse multōs: 574

bonīne an malī sint, id haud quaeritant; rēs   575

magis quaeritur quam clientum fidēs   576

        quoiusmodī clueat.   577

sī est pauper atque haud malus, nēquam habētur,   578

sīn dīues malust, is cliens frūgī habētur.   579

quī nec lēgēs neque aequom bonum usquam colunt,   580

        sollicitōs patrōnōs habent.   581

datum dēnegant quod datum est, lītium plēnī, rapācēs   582

        uirī, fraudulentī,   583

quī aut faenore aut periūriīs habent rem parātam,   584

        mens est in querēlīs.   584a

eīs ubi dīcitur diēs, simul patrōnīs dīcitur.   585

quippe quī prō illīs loquantur, quae male fēcerint: 586

        aut ad populum aut in iūre aut ad iūdicem rēst.   587

Sīcut mē hodiē nimis sollicitum cliens quīdam habuit, neque

    quod uoluī   588

589 quicum = cum quo.
    licitumst = licitum est. perfect of *licet*. "It was not permitted (to
        me) to do what I wanted or with whom (I wanted to do it)."
    attineo, -ere, -tinui, -tentum. to hold, hold back, detain.
    detineo, -ere, -tinui, -tentum. to hold off, keep back, detain, delay.
        The subject of both verbs is the *cliens*.
590 aedilis, -is, m. an aedile (the magistrate before whom certain
        criminal cases were tried).
    facta, -orum, n. pl. deeds, actions.
    plurumi (plurimi), -ae, -a. many, very many.
    pessumus (pessimus), -a, -um. worst, very bad.
591 dixi causam: "I pled his case."
    condicio, -onis, f. an agreement, stipulation, compact, terms.
    tetuli: reduplicated form of *tuli*. "I brought (proposed) terms."
    tortus, -a, -um. twisted, crooked, contorted, distorted.
    confragosus, -a, -um. broken, rough, uneven; hard, difficult.
592 haut = haud. haut plus haut minus: "no more, no less."
    dictum, -i, n. a saying, saying. quam opus fuerat dicto: "than
        there had been need for saying."
    controrsim. (adv.). in opposition.
593 sponsio, -onis, f. a promise; a wager, forfeit (in law suits, a mutual
        agreement between the two parties that the one who loses would pay
        a certain sum to the winner). Reaching an agreement of this sort
        would allow the case of Menaechmus' client to be postponed and
        would allow Menaechmus to return to Erotium's house for lunch.
    qui = is.
    prope haut: "almost didn't."
    praes, praedis, m. surety, bail. (Equivalent to the sum agreed upon
        in the *sponsio*.) Menaechmus was annoyed that after he had argued
        with great difficulty to achieve the *sponsio*, his client balked
        at providing the surety.
594 manufestus (manifestus), -a, -um. clear, apparent, evident; proved by
        direct evidence, exposed.
595 male facta, -orum, n. pl. bad deeds, crimes.
    testis, -is, m. witness.
    adsum, -esse, adfui. to be at, near, present.
    acerrumi = acerrimi.
595a perdo, -ere, -didi, -ditum. to destroy.
596 corrumpo, -ere, -rupi, -ruptum. to destroy, ruin, spoil.
597 meque adeo: "and me too" (may the gods destroy: supplying
        di...perdant from 595a).
597a inspicio, -ere, -spexi, -spectum. to look at.
598 optimus, -a, -um. best.
599a adparo, 1. to prepare.
599 primumst licitum = primum licitum est: "it was first permitted."
    ilico. (adv.). instantly, immediately.
599a propero, 1. to hasten.
600 iratus, -a, -um. angry. iratast = irata est.
600a placo, 1. to quiet, calm, appease, pacify.
601 aufero, auferre, abstuli, ablatum. to take away.

agere aut quīcum licitumst: ita mē attinuit, ita dētinuit.   589

apud aedīlēs prō eius factīs plūrumīsque pessumīsque   590

dīxī causam: condiciōnēs tetulī tortās, confragōsās;   591

haut plūs haut minus, quam opus fuerat dictō, dīxeram

    controrsim, ut   592

sponsiō fieret.

       angrily

    Quid ille? quī prope haut praedem dedit.   593

neg magis manufestum ego hominem umquam ullum tenērī uīdī: 594

omnibus male factīs testēs trēs aderant acerrumī.   595

Dī illum omnēs perdant: ita mihi   595a

hunc hodiē corrūpit diem: 596

mēque adeō, quī hodiē forum   597

umquam oculīs inspexī meīs.   597a

diem corrupī optimum.   598

iussī adparārī prandium,   598a

amīca exspectat mē, sciō.   598b

ubi prīmumst licitum, īlicō   599

properāuī abīre dē forō.   599a

irātast crēdō nunc mihi: 600

hopefully

Plācābit palla quam dedī,   600a

quam hodiē uxōrī abstulī atque dētulī huic Erōtiō.   601

602 nubo, -ere, -psi, -tum. to marry + dat. uiro me malo...nuptam:
      (indirect statement) "that I am married to a bad husband."
    illic = ille + ce.
603 sapio, -ire, -ii. to be sensible, wise.
    *mi = mihi.
    potius. (adv.). rather, instead.
604 ne. (interjection). truly, indeed.
    faenerato. (adv.). with interest. The Matrona means that Menaechmus
      will have to pay for his theft of the *palla* (= *illam*).
    sic datur: "That's the way to give it to him!"
605 *clanculum. (adv.). secretly.
    flagitium, -ii, n. a shameful or disgraceful act or thing.
    potis (supply *esse*) = posse.
606 quid...negoti. partitive genitive.
    men = mene.

PE.   *to MA. triumphantly*

Quid ais?

          MA.   *to PE. indignantly*

            Virō mē malō male nuptam.

                PE. *to MA.*

                    Satin audīs quae illic loquitur?   602

MA.   *to PE.*

Satis.

        ME.I *going toward ER.'s house*

           Sī sapiam, hinc introo abeam, ubi mī bene sit.

               PE. *stepping forward and grabbing ME.I*

                  Manē: male erit potius.   603

MA.   *stepping forward to the other side of ME.I*

Nē illam ēcastor faenerātō abstulistī

                 PE. *aside to MA.*   RECITATIVE

                  Sīc datur.   604

MA.   *to ME.I*

Clanculum tē istaec flāgitia facere censēbās potis?   605

ME.I Quid illuc est, uxor, negōtī?

              MA. Mēn rogās?

                  ME.I Vīn hunc rogem?   606

607   aufer: imperative of *aufero, auferre, abstuli, ablatum, to take away.
      palpatio, -onis, f. a stroking, caressing.
      pergo, -ere, perrexi, perrectum. to go on, continue, proceed.
      quid: why.
608   tristis, -e. sad, unhappy, miserable.
      dissimulo, 1. to pretend, dissemble; to hide, conceal.
609   negotist = negoti est.
      paueo (paveo), -ere, paui. to tremble with fear; to be afraid; to
          fear, dread, be terrified at.
610   nil = nihil.
      equidem. (adv.). truly, indeed.
      pallor, -oris, m. paleness, pallor; terror.
      incutio, -ere, -cussi, -cussum. to strike into.
611   ne. negative with impf. subj.
      comedo, -esse, -edi, -esum. to eat up. ne...comesses: the imperfect
         of the hortatory subjunctive expresses an unfulfilled obligation
         in past time: "you should not have..."
      pergo, -ere, perrexi, perrectum. to go on, continue, proceed.
      in + acc. (here) against.

ME.I nods toward PE. and puts his arms around MA., who pushes him away.

MA. Aufer hinc palpātiōnēs.

     PE. *to MA.*

      Perge tū.

        ME.I *to MA.*

          Quid tū mihi   607

tristis es?

    MA. Tē scīre oportet.

      PE. Scit, sed dissimulat malus. 608

ME.I *to MA.*

Quid negōtīst?

    MA. Pallam...

      ME.I *anxiously*

      Pallam?

        MA. Quīdam pallam...

          PE. *to ME.I*

           Quid pauēs?   609

ME.I Nīl equidem paueō.

      PE. *to ME.I*

        Nisi ūnum: palla pallōrem incutit. 610

at tū nē clam mē comessēs prandium.

        to MA.

        Perge in uirum.   611

612 taceo, -ere, -cui, -citum. to be silent.
    uero (vero). (adv.). indeed, truly.
    nuto, 1. to command by a nod or sign.
613 usquam. (adv.). ever.
    nicto, 1. to wink, blink.
614 confidens, -entis. self-confident, bold, daring; shameless, audacious,
       impudent.
    pernego, 1. to deny completely.
615 adiuro, 1. to swear.
616 illuc. to that person or thing, thereto.
617 *equidem. (adv.). truly, indeed.
    *phrygio, -onis, m. embroiderer.
    refero, -ferre, rettuli, relatum. to bring back.
618 pallast = palla est.
    *taceo, -ere, -cui, -citum. to be silent.
    *quando. (conj.). since.
    memini, -isse. (perfect system with present meaning). to remember.
619 ne. (interjection). truly, indeed.
    qui. (abl.). why.
    misera's = misera es.
    expedio, -ire, -ii, -itum. to set free; to put in order, arrange; to
       disclose, explain.
620 numquis = num aliquis.
    delinquo, -ere, -liqui, -lictum. to fail; to do a wrong, transgress,
       offend.
    ancilla, -ae, f. female slave.
621 responso, 1. to answer, reply; to talk back to.
    eloquere: imperative. "Speak out."
    impune. (adv.). without punishment, with impunity.
    nugae, -arum, f. pl. jokes, nonsense. nugas agere: to be a fool.
622 tristis, -e. sad, unhappy, miserable.
    admodum. (adv.). to the limit; very.
    istuc = istud.

ME.I   *aside to PE., nodding his head*

Nōn tacēs?

      PE. Nōn hercle uērō taceō.

             to MA.

               Nūtat, nē loquar.   612

ME.I   Nōn hercle ego quidem usquam quicquam nūtō neque nictō tibi.   613

PE.   Nihil hōc confidentius, quī, quae uidēs, ea pernegat.   614

ME.I *vehemently, to MA.*

Per Iouem deōsque omnīs adiūrō, uxor, (satin hoc est tibi?)   615

mē istī nōn nūtasse.

      PE. *to ME.I*

             Crēdit iam dē istīs tibi; illūc redī.   616

ME.I Quō ego redeam?

      PE. Equidem ad phrygiōnem censeō: ī pallam refer.   617

ME.I Quae istaec pallast?

      PE. *disgusted*

           Taceō iam, quandō haec rem nōn meminit suam.   618

MA.   *in tears*

Nē ego ēcastor mulier misera.

        ME.I *tenderly, to MA.*

            Quī tū misera's? mī expedī.   619

numquis seruōrum dēlīquit? num ancillae aut seruī tibi   620

responsant? ēloquere: impūnē nōn erit.

        MA. *angrily*

           Nūgās agis.   621

ME.I Tristis admodum es: nōn mī istuc satis placet.

         MA. Nūgās agis.   622

623 certe. (adv.). certainly.
     familiaris, -is, m. servant.
     aliquoi = alicui.
     iratus, -a, -um. angry. irata's = irata es.
624 mihi's = mihi es.
     saltem. (adv.). at least, anyhow.
625 delinquo: see 620.
     em. (interjection). indeed! well! ha!
     rursum. (adv.). = rursus. again.
626 aegrest = aegre est. it is vexing, annoying.
     bellus, -a, -um. pretty, handsome; charming, gallant.
     blandior, -iri, -itus. to flatter, soothe, caress, fondle, coax + dat.
627 potin = potisne. "is it possible?"
     molestus, -a, -um. troublesome, bothersome.
628 sic datur: see 604.
     propero, 1. to hasten. properato: future imperative.
     absens, -entis. absent.
     comedo, -esse, -edi, -esum. to eat up.
629 aedis, -is, f. house.
     corona, -ae, f. wreath.
     derideo, -ere, -si, -sum. to laugh at, mock, deride. derideto:
        future imperative.
     ebrius, -a, -um. drunk.
     tetuli = tuli.
631 tun = tune.
     *uero (vero). (adv.). truly, indeed.

ME.I   Certē familiārium aliquoi īrata's.

                          MA. Nūgās agis.   623

ME.I   Num mihi's īrata saltem?

                  MA. Nunc tū non nūgās agis.   624

ME.I   *with injured innocence*

Nōn edepol dēlīquī quicquam.

                MA. Em rursum nunc nūgās agis.   625

ME.I   *trying to caress MA.*

Dīc, mea uxor, quid tibi aegrēst?

                    PE. *aside to MA.*

                    Bellus blandītur tibi.   626

ME.I   *to PE.*

Potin ut mihi molestus nē sīs? num tē appellō?

                     MA. *to ME.I*

                     Aufer manum.   627

PE.   *to MA.*

Sīc datur.

      to ME.I, indignantly

      Properātō absente mē comesse prandium: 628

post ante aedīs cum coronā mē derīdetō ēbrius.   629

ME.I   Neque edepol ego prandī neque hodiē hūc (*pointing to ER.'s house*)

                    intrō tetulī pedem.   630

PE.   Tūn negās?

      ME.I Negō hercle uērō.

              PE. *aside*

              Nihil hōc homine audācius.   631

632 floreus, -a, -um. made of flowers.
633 asto, -are, -stiti. to stand near; to stand.
     sinciput, -pitis, n. head, brain.
634 peregrinus, -i, m. a stranger, foreigner.
635 quin. (conj.). (here) but, indeed, really, rather.
     ut. (here) after.
     dudum. (adv.). a short time ago, just now.
     diuorto (diverto), -ere, -ti, -sum. to turn away, part, separate.
     demum. (adv.). at length, at last.
636 ulciscor, -i, ultus. to punish. Subjunctive in relative clause of
       characteristic.
637 nescio, -ire, -ii, -itum. not to know, to be ignorant.
638 ipsus = ipse.
     quisnam, quaenam, quidnam. who, which, what?
     narro, 1. to tell, report.
639 quasi. (adv.). as if.
640 O hominem malum: accusative of exclamation.
641 dissimulo, 1. to pretend, dissemble; to hide, conceal.
     celo, 1. to hide, conceal.
     probe. (adv.). well, properly, rightly.

to ME.I, and pointing to ER.'s house

Nōn ego tē modo hīc ante aedīs cum corōnā flōreā 632

uīdī astāre, quom negābās mihi esse sānum sinciput 633

et negābās mē nōuisse, peregrīnum aibās esse tē? 634

ME.I *puzzled*

Quīn ut dūdum dīuortī abs tē, redeō nunc dēmum domum. 635

PE. Nōuī ego tē. nōn mihi censēbās esse, quī tē ulciscerer: 636

omnia hercle uxōrī dīxī.

          ME.I Quid dīxistī?

                  PE. Nesciō. 637

eam ipsus rogā.

    ME.I *to MA.*

        Quid hoc est, uxor? quidnam hic narrāuit tibi? 638

MA. turns away from ME.I.

Quid id est? quid tacēs? quīn dīcis quid sit?

             MA. *to ME.I*

             Quasi tū nesciās, 639

mē rogās.

    ME.I Pol haud rogem tē, sī sciam.

             PE. *aside*

             Ō hominem malum: 640

ut dissimulat.

    to ME.I

Nōn potes cēlāre: rem nōuit probē: 641

642 edicto, 1. to speak out, tell.
     pudet, -uit, puditum est. (impersonal verb). it causes shame.
        nil pudet: "it causes you no shame," "you are ashamed of
        nothing."
643 tua uoluntate: "of your own will."
     profiteor, -eri, -fessus. to admit, confess.
     ades: imperative of *adsum, -esse,* to be present.
644 quid: "why."
     tristis, -e. sad, unhappy, miserable.
     faxo = faciam. Supply *ut* with *scias.*
645 mihist = mihi est.
     surruptast = surrupta est.
646 uiden = uidesne.
     scelestus, -a, -um. wicked, abominable, roguish; (as substantive)
        rogue, scoundrel.
     capto, 1. to try to seize or catch; to try to catch in a crafty
        manner, to try to entrap, entice, allure.
647 profecto. (adv.). actually, really, truly, surely.
     saluos (salvus), -a, -um. safe, preserved.
     foret = esset. subjunctive in a contrary to fact condition.
648 tecumst = tecum est.

omnia hercle ego ēdictāuī.

ME.I Quid id est?

MA. to ME.I

Quandō nīl pudet   642

neque uīs tuā uoluntāte ipse profitērī,

turning toward ME.I

audī atque ades.   643

et quid tristis sim et quid hic mihi dīxerit, faxō sciās.   644

palla mihist domō surrupta.

ME.I with pretended shock

Palla surruptast mihi?   645

PE. to MA.

Vidēn ut tē scelestus captat?

to ME.I

Huic surruptast, nōn tibi: 646

nam profectō tibi surrupta sī esset, salua nunc foret.   647

ME.I to PE.

Nīl mihi tēcumst.

to MA.

Sed tū quid ais?

MA. Palla, inquam, periit domō.   648

ME.I Quis eam surrupuit?

MA. Pol istuc ille scit quī illam abstulit.   649

650 homost = homo est.
      factum: supply est; "it was done."
      nequiter. (adv.). wretchedly, miserably, badly.
651 arguo, -ere, -ui, -utum. to show, prove, declare, assert; to accuse.
652 egomet = ego + emphasizing particle *-met*.
653 egon = egone.
      istic: reinforces the *tu* "you there."
      adfero, -ferre, attuli, allatum. to bring.
      noctua, -ae, f. a night-owl.
655 adiuro, 1. to swear.
656 immo. on the contrary.
      falsus, -a, -um. falsum (as substantive) a falsehood, lie.
      dicere: supply *adiuramus*: "we swear that we are not telling..."
657 illam: i.e., the *palla*.
      condono, 1. to give something to someone, to present.
      sic utendam: "only to be used."

ME.I   Quis is homost?

        MA.   Menaechmus quidam.

                ME.I *with pretended indignation*

                    Edepol factum nequiter.   650

quis is Menaechmust?

        MA.   Tu istic, inquam.

        ME.I   Egone?

          MA.   *sharply*

          Tu.

                ME.I   Quis arguit?   651

MA.   Egomet.

    PE.   Et ego.

        pointing to house of ER.

        Atque huic amicae detulisti Erotio.   652

ME.I   *in disbelief*

Egon dedi?

        MA.   Tu, tu istic, inquam.

                PE.   *to ME.I*

                    Vin adferri noctuam,   653

quae 'tu tu' usque dicat tibi? nam nos iam defessi sumus.   654

ME.I   *to MA.*

Per Iouem deosque omnis adiuro, uxor, (satin hoc est tibi?)   655

non dedisse...

        PE.   *interrupting ME.I*

                Immo hercle uero, nos non falsum dicere.   656

ME.I   *weakly*

Sed ego illam non condonaui, sed sic utendam dedi.   657

658   chlamys, -ydis, f. (Greek word). the chlamys, a broad, woolen upper
      garment worn in Greece.
      foras. (adv.). out of doors, out.
      pallium, -i, n. a Greek cloak or mantle.
659   aequomst = aequom est.
      uestimentum (vestimentum), -i, n. garment.
      muliebris, -e. of or belonging to a woman.
660   uirilis (virilis), -e. of or belonging to a man.
      refero, -ferre, rettuli, relatum. to bring back.
661   faxo = faciam, here followed by future indicative.
      ex re tua: "to your advantage."
662   introeo, -ire, -ii, -itum. to enter.
663   futurumst = futurum est.
      operam dare: to take care for, give attention to, render service to.
664   quid = aliquid.
665   perdo, -ere, -didi, -ditum. to destroy; to lose.
666   di = dei.
      propero, 1. to hasten.
667   plane. (adv.). plainly.
      excido, -ere, -cidi. to fall down or from, to fall out from.
668   male facere + dat. to treat someone badly.
      sese = se.
      excludo, -ere, -si, -sum. to shut out.
669   quasi. as if.
      intromitto, -ere, -misi, -missum. to let in.
      melior, -ius. better.
670   displiceo, -ere, -ui, -itum. to displease.
671   occludo, -ere, -si, -sum. to shut or close up.
672   *dudum. (adv.). just now.
673   redimo, -ere, -emi, -emptum. to buy.
      heus. (interjection). ho! ho there!
      ecquis, ecquid. any.
      ianitor, -oris, m. door-keeper.
674   euoco (evoco), 1. to call out.
      *ostium, -i, n. door.

MA.	Equidem ecastor tuam nec chlamydem dō forās nec pallium	658
	cuiquam ūtendum. mulierem aequomst uestīmentum muliebre	659
	dare forās, uirum uirīle. quīn refers pallam domum?	660
ME.I	Ego faxō referētur.	

MA. Ex rē tuā, ut opīnor, fēceris: 661

nam domum numquam introībis, nisi ferēs pallam simul. 662

turning toward her house

Eō domum

PE. *anxiously to MA.*

Quid mihi futūrumst, quī tibi hanc operam dedī? 663

| MA. | Opera reddētur, quandō quid tibi erit surruptum domō. | 664 |

MA. exits into her house.

PE.	Id quidem edepol numquam erit, nam nihil est, quod perdam, domī.	665
	cum uirō cum uxōre dī uōs perdant. properabō ad forum:	666
	nam ex hāc familiā mē plānē excidisse intellegō.	667

PE. exits to the spectators' right, to the forum.

| ME.I | Male mī uxor sēsē fēcisse censet, quom exclūsit forās, | 668 |
| | quasi nōn habeam, quō intrōmittar, alium meliōrem locum. | 669 |

nodding first toward his own house and then toward Erotium's

Sī tibi displiceō, patiundum, at placuerō huic Erōtiō. 670

quae mē nōn exclūdet ab sē, sed apud sē occlūdet domī. 671

going toward house of ER.

Nunc ībō, ōrabō ut mihi pallam reddat, quam dūdum dedī. 672

aliam illī redimam meliōrem.

knocking on ER.'s door

Heus, ecquis hīc est iānitor? 673

aperīte atque Erōtium aliquis ēuocāte ante ostium. 674

675 aetati tuae = your youthfulness.
676 mi: vocative of *meus*.
   asto, -are, -stiti. to stand near, to stand.
   sequere. imperative.
677 quod: "because of which."
   uolup. (adv.). agreeably, delightfully, pleasurably.
678 *immo. on the contrary.
   amabo te: "please."
679 rescisco, -ere, -iui *or* -ii, -itum. to learn, find out.
   factumst = factum est.
680 redimo, -ere, -emi, -emptum. to buy.
   bis tanta (pecunia): ablative of degree of difference with *pluris*.
      "by twice as much money."
   plus, pluris. more. here; genitive of value with *pallam*: "a *palla*
      of more value by twice as much money."
681 paulo. (adv.). a little.
   prius. (adv.). earlier, before.
682 spinter, -eris, n. bracelet.
   aurifex, -ficis, m. goldsmith.
683 ut...dederis: subjunctive in an exclamatory question.
685 postillac. (adv.). after that.
686 *quia. (conj.). because.
   committo, -ere, -misi, -missum. to give, intrust, commit to. supply:
      tibi pallam et spinter.
   defrudo, 1. to defraud, cheat.
   adfecto, 1. to strive after, pursue, aim at. adfectare uiam: to
      enter on a way in order to reach a certain end; to aim at.
687 rescisco, -ere, -iui *or* -ii, -itum. to learn, find out.
689 tute = emphatic *tu*.
   donum, -i, n. gift. dono: dat. of purpose.
690 reposco, -ere. to demand back.
   utere: imperative.
691 loculus, -i, m. storage chest. (dim. of *locus*, place).
   compingo, -ere, -pegi, -pactum. to join together; to confine, lock up,
      put, conceal.

ER. enters from her house on the spectators' left.

ER. Quis hīc mē quaerit?

      ME.I Sibi inimīcus magis quam aetātī tuae. 675

ER. Mī Menaechme, cūr ante aedīs astās? sequere intrō.

           ME.I Manē. 676

scīn quid est, quod ego ad tē uenīo?

      ER. Sciō, ut tibi ex mē sit uolup. 677

ME.I *caressing ER.*

   Immō edepol pallam illam, amābō tē, quam tibi dūdum dedī, 678

mihi eam redde: uxor resciuit rem omnem, ut factumst, ordine. 679

ego tibi redīmam bis tantā plūris pallam, quam uolēs. 680

ER. *surprised*

   Tibi dedī equidem illam, ad phrygiōnem ut ferrēs, paulō prius 681

et illud spintēr, ut ad aurificem ferrēs, ut fieret nouom. 682

MÉ.I *in disbelief*

   Mihi tū ut dederis pallam et spintēr? numquam factum reperiēs. 683

nam ego quidem postquam illam dūdum tibi dedī atque abiī ad forum, 684

nunc redeō, nunc tē postillāc uideō.

      ER. *becoming annoyed*

        Videō quam rem agis; 685

quia commīsī, ut mē dēfrūdēs, ad eam rem adfectās uiam. 686

ME.I Neque edepol tē dēfrūdandī causā poscō: quīn tibi 687

dīcō uxōrem resciuisse.

      ER. Nec tē ultrō ōrauī ut darēs: 688

tūte ultrō ad mē dētulistī, dedistī eam dōnō mihi: 689

eandem nunc reposcis: patiar. tibi habē, aufer, ūtere 690

uel tū, uel tua uxor, uel etiam in loculōs compingite. 691

692 frustra. (adv.). in deception, in error. ne frustra sis: "Don't
      delude yourself."
693 bene merentem: "deserving well."
     despicatus, -us, m. contempt. habere despicatui: to hold someone in
      contempt, to despise the person.
694 argentum, -i, n. silver; money.
     frustra's = frustra es: you delude, fool yourself.
     ducto, 1. to lead, to take (here in an erotic sense).
695 posthac. (adv.). after this.
     inuenito: future imperative.
     frustratus, -us, m. a deceiving, deception. habere frustratui: to
      deceive, cheat.
696 nimis. (adv.). too.
     iracunde. (adv.). angrily.
     tandem. (adv.). at length, at last, finally.
     heus. (interjection). ho! ho there!
697 redi: imperative of *redeo*.
     asto, -are, -stiti. to stand.
     audeo, -ere, ausus. to have a mind to do something, to be prepared, to
      intend; to dare. here: etiam audes...reuorti: "Won't you please
      come back?"
     reuortor (revertor), -i, -sus. to return.
     mea...gratia: "for my sake."
698 occludo, -ere, -si, -sum. to shut or close up.
     exclusus, -a, -um. shut out. exclusissumus = exclusissimus.
700 consulo, -ere, -lui, -ltum. to ask someone's advice about something
     (here with two accusatives).

	tū hūc post hunc diem pedem intrō nōn ferēs, nē frustrā sīs.	692
	quandō tū mē bene merentem tibi habēs despicātuī,	693
	nisi ferēs argentum, frustrā's; mē ductāre nōn potes.	694
	aliam posthāc inuenītō, quam habeās frustrātuī.	695

ER. moves toward her house to go inside

ME.I Nimis īracundē hercle tandem. heus tū, tibi dīcō, manē. 696

redī. etiamne astās? etiam audēs meā reuortī gratiā? 697

ER. goes inside and slams the door in ME.I's face.

Abiit intrō, occlūsit aedīs.

discouraged

Nunc ego sum exclusissumus: 698

neque domī neque apud amīcam mihi iam quicquam crēditur. 699

ībō et consulam hanc rem amīcōs, quid faciendum censeant. 700

ME.I exits to the spectators' right, to the forum.

701 *nimis. (adv.). too.
  stulte. (adv.). foolishly.
  marsuppium, -ii, n. pouch, purse.
702 argentum, -i, n. silver; money.
  concredo, -ere, -didi, -ditum. to intrust, give to.
703 inmergo, -ere, -si, -sum. to dip, plunge, immerse.
  aliquo. (adv.). somewhere.
  sese = se.
  ganeum, -i, n. an eating-house, cook-shop.
704 prouiso (proviso), -ere. to come or go forth to see or to look out
      for.
705 saluos (saluus), -a, -um. saved, safe.
  *refero, -ferre, rettuli, relatum. to bring back.
706 demiror, -ari, -atus. to wonder.
  *ambulo, 1. to walk.
707 *adeo, -ire, -ii, -itum. to go to, approach.
  *dictum, -i, n. word.
708 pudet, -uit, puditum est. (impersonal verb). it causes shame.
      te pudet: "it causes you shame," "you are ashamed."
  prodeo, -ire, -ii, -itum. to come forth.
  conspectus, -us, m. sight, view.
709 flagitium hominis: see 489.
  ornatus, -us, m. garment.
710 agito, 1. to put in motion, drive, impel; disturb, vex, trouble.
  impudens, -entis. shameless, impudent.
711 muttio, -ire, -ivi. to mutter, mumble.
  uerbum (verbum), -i, n. word.
  audeo, -ere, ausus. to have a mind to do something, to be prepared,
      to intend; to dare.
712 tandem. (adv.). at length, at last, finally. Quid tandem: "What in
      the world?"
  admitto, -ere, -misi, -missum. to admit; to become guilty of, per-
      petrate, commit (a wrongdoing). Quid...admisi in me: "What am I
      guilty of?"
713 audacia, -ae, f. boldness.
714 Hecuba, -ae, f. Hecuba, wife of Priam, was changed into a bitch after
      snarling at the Thracians when they attacked her after she had
      blinded their king who had killed her son.
  quapropter. (adv.). for what reason, why.
  canis, -is, m. or f. dog, bitch.
715 Graii, -orum, m. pl. Greeks.
  praedico, 1. to make known, say, relate, declare.

ACT V

ME.II enters from the spectators' left, from the harbor, carrying the palla.

ME.II   Nimis stultē dūdum fēcī, quom marsuppium   701

Messēniōnī cum argentō concrēdidī: 702

inmersit aliquō sēsē, crēdō, in gāneum.   703

MA. enters from her house and is not seen by ME.II

MA.   Prōuīsam, quam mox uir meus redeat domum.   704

seeing ME.II

Sed eccum uideō. salua sum, pallam refert.   705

ME.II   *to himself*

Dēmīror, ubi nunc ambulet Messēniō.   706

MA.   *to herself*

Adībō atque hominem accipiam quibus dictīs meret.   707

to ME.II as she walks up to him

Nōn tē pudet prodīre in conspectum meum,   708

flāgitium hominis, cum istōc ornātu?

ME.II   *startled*

Quid est?   709

quae tē rēs agitat, mulier?

MA.   Etiamne, impudens,   710

muttīre uerbum ūnum audēs aut mēcum loquī?   711

ME.II   Quid tandem admīsī in mē, ut loquī nōn audeam?   712

MA.   Rogās mē? ō hominis impudentem audāciam.   713

ME.II   Nōn tū scīs, mulier, Hecubam quāpropter canem   714

Graiī esse praedicābant?

MA.   Nōn equidem sciō.   715

717   ingero, -ere, -gessi, -gestum. to carry into; to inflict upon; to
        pour out against. omnia mala: all sorts of insults.
     aspicio, -ere, -spexi, -spectum. to behold, look at, see.

718   iure. (adv.). rightly.
     appellarist = appellari est.
     canes = canis (nom. sing.).

719   flagitium, -ii, n. a shameful or disgraceful act or thing.
     perpetior, -i, -pessus. to suffer, endure.

720   med = me.
     aetatem: accusative of extent of time: "thoughout my life."
     uiduos (viduus), -a, -om. without a husband, widowed.
     mauelim: present subjunctive of *malo*.

722   Quid id ad me (attinet): "How does that pertain to me?"
     nuptus, -a, -um. married.

723   sis abitura: "you are about to depart."
     itast = ita est.

724   peregrinus, -a, -um. foreigner, stranger.
     aduenio (advenio), -ire, -ueni, -uentum. to arrive.
     narro, 1. to tell.
     fabula, -ae, f. story, tale.

725   praeterhac. (adv.). beyond this.

726   uiduos (viduus), -a, -om. without a husband, widowed.
     quam: supply *potius* "rather" before *uiuam*. "but that I would rather
       live...than..."
     perfero, -ferre, -tuli, -latum. to bear through; to suffer, endure.

727   mea...causa: "as far as I am concerned."
     uiuito (vivito): future imperative.

728   uel (vel). even.
     usque dum. as long as.
     optineo = obtineo.

730   attineo, -ere, -tinui, -tentum. to hold to or near.
     pudet, -uit, puditum est. it causes shame.

731   heu. (interjection). oh! ah!
     multum. (adv.). very.
     mala's = mala es.

732   tun = tune.
     *audeo, -ere, ausus. to have a mind to do something, to be prepared,
       to intend; to dare.

733   concinno, 1. to fit together, set right, repair.

734   ne. (interjection). truly, indeed. Matrona begins to expostulate
     against what Menaechmus has just said, but then changes her mind
     and her sentence.

735   *flagitium, -ii, n. a shameful or disgraceful act or thing.

736   i: imperative of *eo*.

737   ita rem esse: "that things are so."
     dicito: future imperative.

ME.II	Quia idem faciebat Hecuba, quod tū nunc facis.	716
	omnia mala ingerebat, quemquem aspexerat:	717
	itaque adeō iūre coepta appellārīst canēs.	718
MA.	*indignant*	
	Nōn ego istaec flāgitia possum perpetī:	719
	nam mēd aetātem uiduam esse māuelim,	720
	quam istaec flāgitia tua patī, quae tū facis.	721
ME.II	Quid id ad mē, tū tē nuptam possīs perpetī	722
	an sīs abitūra ā tuō uirō? an mōs hīc itast,	723
	peregrīnō ut aduenientī narrent fābulās?	724
MA.	Quās fābulās? nōn, inquam, patiar praeterhāc.	725
	quīn uidua uīuam, quam tuōs mōrēs perferam.	726
ME.II	Meā quidem hercle causā uidua uīuitō	727
	vel usque dum regnum optinēbit Iuppiter.	728
MA.	*pointing to the* palla	
	At mihi hanc negābās dūdum surrupuisse tē,	729
	nunc eandem ante oculōs attinēs: nōn tē pudet?	730
ME.II	Heu hercle, mulier multum et audax et mala's.	731
	tūn tibi hanc surruptam dīcere audēs, quam mihi	732
	dedit alia mulier, ut concinnandam darem?	733
MA.	Nē istuc mēcastor -- iam patrem arcessam meum	734
	atque eī narrābō tua flāgitia quae facis.	735
	calling into her house to a slave	
	Ī, Deciō, quaere meum patrem, tēcum simul	736
	ut ueniat ad mē: ita rem esse dīcitō.	737

738 aperiam: here in sense of "disclose," "make known."
 sanan = sanane
739 aurum, -i, n. gold, jewelry.
740 suppilo, 1. to steal.
 tuae uxori. dative of separation.
741 degero, -ere. to carry off.
 satin = satisne.
 recte. (adv.). rightly, correctly.
 fabulor, -ari, -atus. to speak, say.
742 quaeso, -ere, -ii. to beg, pray, beseech.
 monstro, 1. to show, point out, indicate. (imperative here).
 bibo, -ere, bibi, bibitum. to drink. quod bibam: "something I
    might drink" (to make me able to put up with your impertinence).
743 qui = *quo*, introducing a relative clause of purpose.
 perpetior, -i, -pessus. to suffer, endure.
 petulantia, -ae, f. sauciness, impudence, petulance.
744 med = me.
 arbitrere = arbitreris, 2nd person sing., subjunctive of *arbitror*,
    "to think."
 *nescio, -ire, -ii, -itum. not to know, to be ignorant.
745 simitu. (adv.). at once, at the same time, together.
 Porthaon, -onis, m. the grandfather of Deianira, wife of Heracles.
746 *derideo, -ere, -si, -sum. to laugh at, scoff at, deride.
747 *aduenio (advenio), -ire, -i, -uentum. to come.
 respicio, -ere, -spexi, -spectum. to look back or behind.
748 nouistin = nouistine.
 Calchas, -antis (abl. Calcha). Calchas, the seer of the Greeks during
    the Trojan War.
751 auos (avus), -i, m. grandfather.
 adduco, -ere, -xi, -ctum. to bring.
752 pariter. (adv.). equally.
 soleo, -ere, -itus. to be accustomed to + infinitive (supply *facere*).
    Matrona thinks that Menaechmus is simply up to his usual tricks.

A slave enters from the house and exits to the spectators' right;
MA. continues to upbraid ME.II.

MA.   Iam ego aperiam istaec tua flāgitia.

                         ME.II Sānan es?   738

quae mea flāgitia?

                 MA.   Pallam atque aurum meum   739

domō suppīlās tuae uxōrī et tuae   740

dēgeris amīcae. satin haec rectē fābulor?   741

ME.II Quaesō hercle, mulier, sī scīs, monstrā quod bibam, 742

     tuam quī possim perpetī petulantiam.   743

     quem tū mēd hominem arbitrēre, nesciō: 744

     ego tē simītū nōuī cum Porthāone.   745

MA.   Sī mē dērīdēs, at pol illum nōn potes,   746

pointing off stage to the spectators' right

patrem meum, quī hūc aduenit.

Senex, *the matrona's father, enters with Decio from the*
spectators' right.

            MA. *to ME.II*

               Quīn respicis?   747

nōuistīn tū illum?

                ME.II Nōuī cum Calchā simul: 748

eōdem diē illum uīdī, quō tē ante hunc diem.   749

MA.   Negās nōuisse mē? negās patrem meum?   750

ME.II Idem hercle dīcam, sī auom uīs addūcere.   751

ME.II walks away from MA., toward spectators' left.

MA.   Ēcastor pariter hoc atque aliās rēs solēs.   752

753 ut aetas meast: "as is my age," i.e., as quickly as my age permits me
 to go. meast = mea est.
 ut hoc usus factost: "as there is need in this business," i.e., as
 the occasion requires. factost = facto est.
754 gradus, -us, m. step, pace.
 profero, -ferre, -tuli, -latum. to carry or bring forth.
 progredior, -i, -gressus. to go forth, proceed.
 propero, 1. to hasten.
755 "But I am not deceived as to how easy it is for me."
756 pernicitas, -atis, f. nimbleness, agility, swiftness.
 consero, -ere, -seui, -situm. to sow or plant with. Here,
 metaphorically = "I am full of" + abl.
757 senectus, -utis, f. old age, senility.
 onustus, -a, -um. loaded, laden, burdened.
 uires (vires): pl. of *uis.* in pl. = "strength."
758 reliquere = reliquerunt.
 aetas: "old age."
 mers = merx, -cis, f. goods, wares, merchandise, cargo.
 ergost = ergo est.
759 plurumi (plurimi), -ae, -a. most; many.
 pessumus (pessimus), -a, -um. worst.
 adfero, -ferre, attuli, allatum. to bring.
760 autumo, 1. to affirm, assert, say, name.
 sermo, -onis, m. talk, conversation, discourse. sermost = sermo est.
761 pectus, -oris, n. breast; heart.
 cor, cordis, n. heart.
 curaest = curae est: dative of purpose; "it is (for) a care to me."
762 quisnam, quaenam, quidnam. who, which, what.
762a expeto, -ere, -ii, -itum. to seek.
 sese = se.
763 mihi certius facit: "does she make it more certain to me" = "does she
 inform me." Cf. the usual idiom, *certiorem facere aliquem,* "to
 inform someone."
763a accerso, -ere = arcesso, -ere, iui, -itum. to summon.
764 uerum (verum). (adv.). truly.
 propemodum. (adv.). nearly, almost.
 siet = sit.
765 litigium, -i, n. dispute, quarrel, strife.
 aliqui, aliqua, aliquod. some.
766 soleo, -ere, -itus. to be accustomed.
 subseruio (subservio), -ire. to be subject to, to serve.
767 dos, -otis, f. dowry.
 fretus, -a, -um. relying on, trusting to + abl.
 ferox, -ocis. bold, courageous, headstrong, fierce, insolent.

762ff. Is Senex's attitude toward woman's role in marriage consistent with
 that of Menaechmus I (cf. 110ff.)? What social practice does he hold
 responsible for women's impertinence? Of what offense does his
 father-in-law consider Menaechmus I guilty? What does his judgment
 convey about standards of right and wrong?

SE. *querulously to himself as he walks slowly, leaning on his cane,*
not seeing MA. or ME.II

	SONG
Vt aetās meast atque ut hōc ūsus factōst,	753
gradum prōferam, prōgredīrī properābō.	754
sed id quam mihi facile sit, haud sum falsus.	755
nam pernīcitās dēserit: consitus sum	756
senectūte: onustum gerō corpus: uīrēs	757
relīquēre. ut aetās mala est! mers mala ergōst.	758
nam rēs plūrumās pessumās, quom aduenit, ad-	759
fert, quās sī autumem omnīs, nimis longus sermōst.	760
sed haec rēs mihi in pectore et corde cūraest,	761
quidnam hoc sit negōtī, quod sīc fīlia	762
repentē expetit mē, ut ad sēsē īrem.	762a
nec, quid id sit, mihi certius facit, quid	763
uelit, quid mē accersat.	763a
uērum propemodum iam sciō, quid siet reī:	764
crēdō cum uirō lītigium nātum esse aliquod.	765
ita istaec solent, quae uirōs subseruīre	766
sibi postulant, dōte frētae, ferōcēs.	767

768 illi: i.e., the husbands.
     abstineo, -ere, -ui, -tentum. to keep off or away, to abstain from,
       be free from.
     culpa, -ae, f. fault, blame.
769 uerum (verum). (conj.). but. "But (there is) a limit..."
     uerumst = uerum est.
     quoad. (adv.). how far.
770 accerso, -ere. to summon.
771 commissum, -i, n. a transgression, offense, fault.
     iurgium, -i, n. a quarrel, strife, dispute. *commissi* and *iurgi* are
       partitive genitives dependent on *quid = aliquid*. iurgist =
       iurgi est.
772 eampse = eam.
773 *tristis, -e. sad, sorrowful, unhappy.
775 aduorsum (adversum). (adv.). opposite to, against, toward. aduorsum
       ire: to approach.
     salue (salve): imperative. "Greetings!" salueo, -ere. to be well
       or in good health.
776 saluos (salvus), -a, -om. saved, preserved, safe, well.
     salue (salve). (adv.). well, in good health, in good condition or
       circumstances. saluen = saluene.
     accerso, -ere. to summon. supply *me*.
777 *iratus, -a, -um. angry.
     desisto, -ere, -stiti, -stitum. to stand apart.
778 nescioquid. I don't know what = something.
     uelitor (velitor), -ari, -atus. to fight like light troops *(uelites)*,
       to skirmish. *nescioquid* is internal accusative: "You've had
       some skirmish."
779 culpa, -ae. f. blame.
     logos, -i, m. (Greek word). word. (acc. pl. here).
780 nusquam. (adv.). nowhere.
     delinquo, -ere, -liqui, -lictum. to fail, commit a fault, do wrong,
       transgress.
     primum. (adv.). in the first place.
     absoluo (absolvo), -ere, -ui, -utum. to loosen from, set free. "I
       free you from this (suspicion)."
781 uerum (verum). (conj.). but.
     duro, 1. to be hard; to be patient, to endure.
782 proin. (adv.). just so; hence, therefore.
     abduco, -ere, -xi, -ctum. to lead away.
     autem. (here an emphasizing word). indeed. autemst = autem est.
     ludibrium, -ii, n. a mockery, derision; a laughing-stock. dative
       of purpose with *habeor*: "I am considered a (mere) laughing-
       stock."

et illī quoque haud abstinent saepe culpā,   768

uērumst modus tamen, quoad patī uxōrem oportet.   769

nec pol fīlia umquam patrem accersit ad sē,   770

nisi aut quid commissī aut iurgīst causa.   771

Sed id quicquid est, iam sciam.

               catching sight of MA. and ME.II

               Atque eccam eampse   772

ante aedīs et eius uirum uideō tristem.   773

id est, quod suspicābar.   .   774

appellābō hanc.

         MA. *approaching SE.*

                                     RECITATIVE

               Ibō aduorsum. saluē multum, mī pater.   775

SE.   Salua sīs. saluēn adueniō? saluēn accersī iubēs?   776

quid tū tristis es?

         glancing at ME.II

               Quid ille autem abs tē īratus dēstitit?   777

nescioquid uōs uēlitātī estis inter uōs duōs.   778

to MA. and ME.II

Loquere, ūter meruistis culpam, paucīs, nōn longōs logōs.   779

MA.   Nusquam equidem quicquam dēlīquī: hōc prīmum tē absoluō, pater: 780

uērum uīuere hīc nōn possum neque durāre ullō modō: 781

proin tū mē hinc abdūcās.

         SE. Quid istuc autemst?

               MA. Lūdibriō, pater,   782

783 quoi = cui.
784 litigium, -i, n. dispute, quarrel, strife.
quotiens. (adv.). how many times.
tandem. (adv.). (in interrogative clauses). pray, pray now, now,
     then.
edico, -ere, -xi, -ctum. to declare.
785 caueo (caveo), -ere, caui, cautum. to be on one's guard. to watch
     out, beware.
quaerimonia, -ae, f. a complaint.
786 qui. (adv.). how.
interrogo, 1. to ask.
788 quotiens. (adv.). how many times, how often.
monstro, 1. to show, point out.
morem gerere + dat. lit.: to bear the custom or fashion to or for a
     person; to humor, gratify, obey.
789 ne id obserues: "that you should not observe."
790 proxumus (proximus), -a, -um. nearest. ex proxumo: next door.
sane. (adv.). soundly, healthily, well, truly, certainly, very.
sapio, -ire, -ii. to have taste; to be sensible, wise.
791 industria, -ae, f. industry, activity, diligence.
faxo = faciam. (parenthetical). "I'll warrant," "I'll assure you."
792 poto, 1. to drink.
tua...causa. for your sake.
minus. (adv.). less.
793 illic. (adv.). there.
alibi. (adv.). elsewhere.
libet, libuit, libitum est. it pleases.
impudentia, -ae, f. shamelessness, impudence. impudentiast =
     impudentia est.
794 una opera: in the same manner, at the same time.
promitto, -ere, -misi, -missum. to promise. ad cenam promittere:
     to accept an invitation out to dinner. "at the same time you
     might as well demand to prohibit him from dining out."
795 neu. and that not.
alienum: i.e., from outside the household.
apud se: at his house.
seruiren = seruirene. seruio (servio), -ire, -ii, -itum. to be a
     servant or slave.
796 pensum, -i, n. (from pendo, -ere, to weigh out). the wool weighed
     out to a slave to spin in a day.
797 ancilla, -ae, f. female slave.
sedeo, -ere, sedi, sessum. to sit.
lana, -ae, f. wool.
caro, -ere. to card.
798 aduocatus (advocatus), -i, m. a legal counsellor, advocate, attorney.
adduco, -ere, -xi, -ctum. to bring.

habeor.

    SE.   Vnde?

             MA. *pointing to ME.II*

                Ab illō, quoi mē mandāuistī, meō uirō.   783

SE.   *aside*

Ecce autem lītigium.

        to MA.

        Quotiens tandem ego ēdīxī tibi,   784

ut cauerēs, neuter ad mē īrētis cum querimōniā?   785

MA.   Quī ego istuc, mī pater, cauēre possum?

               SE. Mēn interrogās?   786

MA.   Nisi nōn uīs.

          SE. Quotiens monstrāuī tibi, uirō ut mōrem gerās,   788

quid ille faciat, nē id obseruēs, quō eat, quid rērum gerat. 789

MA.   At enim ille hinc amat meretrīcem ex proxumō.

               SE. Sānē sapit,   790

atque ob istanc industriam etiam faxō amābit amplius.   791

MA.   Atque ibī pōtat.

          SE. Tuā quidem ille causā pōtābit minus,   792

sī illīc, sīue alibī libēbit? quae haec, malum, impudentiast? 793

ūnā operā prohibēre, ad cēnam nē prōmittat, postulēs,   794

neu quemquam accipiat aliēnum apud sē. seruīren tibi   795

postulās uirōs? dare ūnā operā pensum postulēs,   796

inter ancillās sedēre iubeās, lānam cārere.   797

MA.   *resentfully*

Nōn equidem mihi tē aduocātum, pater, addūxī, sed uirō: 798

799   hinc. (adv.). from this place, hence; on this side, here.
      illim. (adv.). thence, from that place.
      causam dicere: to plead a case.
      quid = aliquid.
      delinquo, -ere, -liqui, -lictum. to fail, commit a fault, do wrong,
         transgress.
800   multo *and* tanta (opera) *modify* amplius. "very much more."
      accuso, 1. to accuse.
801   auratus, -a, -um. furnished with gold.
      uestitus (vestitus), -a, -um. clothed.
      ancilla, -ae, f. female slave.
      penus, -us, m. store or provision of food; provisions.
802   recte. (adv.). rightly, properly.
      praehibeo, -ere. to hold forth, furnish, supply.
      melius...est. it is better.
803   suppilo, 1. to steal.
      *aurum, -i, n. gold.
      arca, -ae, f. box, chest.
804   despolio, 1. to rob, plunder, despoil.
      ornamentum, -i, n. ornament, jewelry.
      degero, -ere. to carry away, carry off.
806   insons, -ntis. guiltless, innocent.
      insimulo, 1. to charge, accuse, blame (usually falsely).
807   *spinter, -eris, n. bracelet.
      rescisco, -ere, -ivi *or* -ii, -itum. to learn, find out.
808   factumst = factum est.
      adloquor, -i, -cutus. to speak to.
809   disserto, 1. to discuss, argue, debate.
810   desisto, -ere, -stiti, -stitum. to stand off, stand apart.
811   summus, -a, -um. highest.
812   testis, -is, m. witness.
      quoius = cuius. "or of what of all things?"
813   male facere + dat. to treat badly.
      arguo, -ere, -ui, -utum. to accuse, charge with.
814   peiero, 1. to swear falsely.
816   habito, 1. to live.
      penetro, 1. to put, place, set something into anything.

hinc stās, illim causam dīcis.

SE. Sī ille quid dēlīquerit,   799

multō tantā illum accusābō, quam tē accusāuī, amplius.   800

quandō tē aurātam et uestītam bene habet, ancillās, penum 801

rectē praehibet, melius sānam est, mulier, mentem sūmere. 802

MA.   At ille suppīlat mihi aurum et pallās ex arcīs domō: 803

me despoliat, mea ornamenta clam ad meretrīcēs dēgerit. 804

SE.   Male facit, sī istuc facit: sī nōn facit, tū male facis, 805

quae insontem insimulēs.

MA. Quīn etiam nunc habet pallam, pater, 806

et spintēr, quod ad hanc dētulerat, nunc, quia rēsciuī, refert. 807

SE.   Iam ego ex hōc, ut factumst, scībō.

walking over to ME.I

Ibō ad hominem atque adloquar.   808

to ME.II

Dīc mī istuc, Menaechme, quod uōs dissertātis, ut sciam. 809

quid tū tristis es? quid illa autem īrāta abs tē dēstitit? 810

ME.II   *vehemently*

Quisquis es, quicquid tibi nōmen est, senex, summum Iouem 811

deōsque dō testīs . . .

SE. Quā dē rē aut quoius reī rērum omnium? 812

ME.II   Mē neque istī male fēcisse mulieri, quae mē arguit 813

hanc domō ab sē surrupuisse atque abstulisse.

MA. *angrily interrupting ME.II*

Pēierat.   814

ME.II   *continuing to SE.*

Sī ego intrā aedīs huius umquam, ubī habitat, penetrāuī pedem, 816

817 exopto, 1. to wish, desire.
818 sanun = sanusne.
819 infero, -ferre, -tuli, -latum. to bring in.
820 tun = tune.
    med = me.
822 quo = aliquo. (adv.). to some place or other.
    emigro, 1. to depart from a place, to emigrate. emigrasti =
        emigravisti.
    concede huc: "come over here."
823 exmigrastis = exmigrauistis.
    *obsecro, 1. to beg, ask.
824 profecto. (adv.). actually, indeed, truly, surely, certainly.
    ludo, -ere, -si, -sum. to play; to make sport of a person.
    non tu tenes: "don't you get it?" "don't you understand?"
825 iocor, -ari, -atus. to jest, joke. iocatu's = iocatus es.
    nunc hanc rem gere: "now get back to business."

omnium hominum exoptō ut fīam miserōrum miserrimus.   817

SE.   *to ME.II*

Sānun es, quī istuc exoptēs, aut negēs tē umquam pedem   818

in eās aedīs intulisse ubī habitās, insānissime?   819

ME.II   *to SE. and pointing to ME.I's house*

Tūn senex, ais habitāre mēd in illīsce aedibus?   820

SE.   *to ME.II*

Tūn negās?

> ME.II   *to SE.*
>
> Negō hercle uērō.
>
>> SE.   *to ME.II*
>>
>> Immō hercle nōn uērē negās,   821

nisi quō nocte hāc ēmigrastī.

>> *to MA.*
>>
>> Tū concēde hūc, fīlia.   822

MA. comes toward SE.

SE.   *to MA.*

Quid tū ais? num hinc exmigrastis?

> MA.   *to SE.*
>
> Quem in locum aut quam ob rem, obsecrō?   823

SE.   *to MA.*

Nōn edepol sciō.

> MA.   *to SE.*
>
> Profectō lūdit tē hic: nōn tū tenēs?   824

SE.   *to ME.II*

Iam uērō, Menaechme, satis iocātu's: nunc hanc rem gere.   825

826 *quaeso, -ere, -ii. to beg, pray, ask.
    tecumst = tecum est.
    homo's = homo es.
827 molestia, -ae, f. trouble, annoyance. quae mihi molestiaest: double
        dative: "who is annoying to me." molestiaest = molestiae est.
    quoquo modo: "in whatever way" = "in every way possible."
828 uiden = uidesne.
    uireo (vireo), -ere, -ui. to be green.
    uiridis (viridis), -e. green.
    exorior, -iri, -ortus. to come forth, to rise.
    colos, -oris, m. color.
829-830 tempora, -um, n. pl. the temples of the head.
    scintillo, 1. to sparkle, glitter, gleam, flash.
831 melior, melius. better. meliust = melius est.
    *insanio, -ire, -ii, -itum. to be insane.
    praedico, 1. to say, state, declare.
832 med = me.
    adsimulo, 1. to pretend.
    absterreo, -ere, -ui, -itum. to frighten away.
833 pandiculor, -ari. to stretch oneself.
    oscitor, -ari. to gape.
834 nata, -ae, f. daughter.
    quam...longissime: "as far as possible."
835 euhoe. (Greek word; interjection). a shout of joy at celebrations of
        Dionysus.
    Bromius, -ii, m. (Greek word: "the noisy one"). a name for Bacchus
        or Dionysus.
    uenor (venor), -ari, -atus. to hunt. uenatum: supine expressing
        purpose.
837 laeuos (laevus), -a, -om. left. ab laeua (manu).
    rabiosus, -a, -um. raving, wild, mad, rabid.
    femina, -ae, f. woman.
    adseruo (adservo), 1. to watch over, protect, guard.
    canis, -is, m. or f. dog.
838 poste = post.
    hircus, -i, m. he-goat.
    alus: this word is a modern emendation where the manuscripts have the
        meaningless *ircosalus*. alus: "smelling of garlic."
        cf. alium, -ii, n. garlic. The word *alus* does not occur else-
        where.
839 perdo, -ere, -didi, -ditum. to destroy, ruin.
    innocens, -entis. innocent.
    falsus, -a, -um. false.
    testimonium, -ii, n. testimony.
840 uae (vae). (interjection). woe + dat.
    Apollo. Greek god of prophecy.
    oraclum, -i, n. oracle.
841 exuro, -ere, -ussi, -ustum. to burn out.
    lampada, -ae, f. (Greek word). torch.
    ardens, -entis. on fire, burning.

ME.II   *impatiently, to SE.*

      Quaesō, quid mihi tēcumst? unde aut quis tū homō's? quid dēbeō   826

      tibi aut adeō istī, quae mihi molestiaest quōquō modō?   827

MA.   *to SE. and pointing to ME.II*

      Vidēn tū illī oculōs uirēre? ut uiridis exoritur colōs   828

      ex temporibus atque fronte: ut oculī scintillant, uidē.   829, 830

ME.II   *aside*

      Quid mihi meliust quam, quandō illī mē insānīre praedicant,   831

      ego mēd adsimulem insānīre, ut illōs ā mē absterream?   832

MA.   *to SE.*

      Vt pandiculans oscitātur. quid nunc faciam, mī pater?   833

SE.   *retreating away from ME.II*

      Concēde hūc, mea nāta, ab istōc quam potes longissimē.   834

ME.II   *charging toward them and pretending to hear a god's command*

      Euhoe atque euhoe, Bromie, quō mē in siluam uēnātum uocās?   835

      audiō, sed nōn abīre possum ab hīs regiōnibus.   836

      pointing to MA.

      Ita illa mē ab laeuā rabiōsa fēmina adseruat canis.   837

      pointing to SE.

      Poste autem illīc hircus alus, quī saepe aetāte in suā   838

      perdidit cīuem innocentem falsō testimōniō.   839

SE.   Vae capitī tuō.

         ME.II   *as if possessed by Apollo*

             Ecce Appollō mihi ex ōraclō imperat,   840

     charging at MA.

    ut ego illī oculōs exūram lampadīs ardentibus.   841

842   minor, -ari, -atus. to threaten.
843   ei. (exclamation). ah! woe! ei mihi: ah me! woe is me!
      ultro. (adv.). on the other side; on their side.
844   heus. (interjection). hey there.
      huc. (adv.). hither.
      cito, 1. to summon.
845   adduco, -ere, -xi, -ctum. to bring.
      qui...tollant: relative clause of purpose.
      deuincio (devincio), -ire, -nxi, -nctum. to bind fast, tie up.
846   turba, -ae, f. disturbance. turbarum: partitive gen. with *quid*.
      quid = aliquid.
      haereo, -ere, haesi, haesum. to stick, cling, be fixed; to stick fast.
         be brought to a stand-still, be perplexed, at a loss.
847   ni = nisi.
      aliqui, aliqua, aliquod. some.
848   pugnus, -i, m. fist. dat. with *parcere*.
      uoto (voto), 1. = ueto, 1. to forbid. The subject of *uotas* is
         Apollo (850).
      os, oris, n. mouth; face. "You forbid me to spare my fists in any
         way against the face of this man."
849   ni = nisi.
      abscedo, -ere, -cessi, -cessum. to go away, depart.
      crux, -ucis, f. see line 66.
850   quantum potest: "as quickly as possible."
851   obtundo, -ere, -tudi, -tusum. to strike or beat against; to beat.
      adseruo (adservo), 1. to watch, guard.

MA. *frightened*

Periī, mī pater: minātur mihi oculōs exūrere.   842

ME.II *aside*

Ei mihi, insānīre mē aiunt, ultrō quom ipsī insāniunt.   843

SE. *to MA.*

Fīlia, heus.

    MA. Quid est?

       SE. Quid agimus? quid, sī ego hūc seruōs citō?   844

ibō, addūcam quī hunc hinc tollant et domī dēuinciant,   845

prius quam turbārum quid faciat amplius.

        ME.II *aside*

              Enim haereō.   846

nī occupō aliquod mihi consilium, hī domum mē ad sē auferent.   847

ME.II rushes again at MA., shouting as if possessed.

ME.II Pugnīs mē uotās in huius ōre quicquam parcere,   848

nī ā meīs oculīs abscēdat in malam magnam crucem.   849

faciam quod iubēs, Apollō.

       SE. *to MA.*

          Fuge domum quantum potest,   850

nē hic tē obtundat.

    MA. *to SE.*

       Fugiō. amābō, adseruā istunc, mī pater,   851

nē quō hinc abeat.

      to herself

      Sumne ego mulier misera, quae illaec audiō?   852

        MA. exits into her house.

853 haud male: "not at all badly," "pretty nicely."
    amoueo (amoveo), -ere, -moui, -motum. to move someone or something
        away.
    impurus, -a, -um. unclean, filthy, foul.
854 barbatus, -a, -um. bearded.
    tremulus, -a, -um. shaking, quaking, trembling.
    Tithonus, -i, m. son of Laomedon, lover of Aurora, he was given im-
        mortality but not eternal youth; after reaching a decrepit old
        age, he was changed into a cicada.
    clueo, -ere. to be named; called; to be known as the son of someone
        (abl.).
    Cygnus, -i, m. the Swan. The allusion is unknown.
855 memburm, -i, n. limb.
    os, ossis, n. bone.
    artus, -us, m. (pl. in neuter: *artua*). a joint; pl. the limbs.
856 comminuo, -ere, -ui, -utum. to break into pieces, to crush.
    scipio, -onis, m. a staff.
857 propius. (adv.). nearer.
858 securis, -is, f. an axe.
    anceps, -cipitis. double-headed.
859 os, ossis, n. bone. osse fini: abl. absolute; "with the bone as
        the end" = "as far as the bone."
    dedolo, 1. to hew.
    assulatim. (adv.). in splinters, piecemeal. (assula, -ae, f. a
        splinter, shaving).
    uiscera (viscera), -um, n. pl. the inner organs.
860 enim uero (vero). to be sure, certainly, indeed.
    praecaueo (praecaveo), -ere, -caui, -cautum. to guard against before-
        hand. -umst = -um est.
    adcuro, 1. to take care of.
861 sane. (adv.). truly, certainly, very.
    minor, -ari, -atus. to threaten.
    faxit = faciat.
863 indomitus, -a, -um. untamed, fierce, wild.
    ferox, -ocis. wild, fierce, untamed.
    currus, -us, m. chariot.
    inscendo, -ere, -scendi, -scensum. to step into, mount.
864 protero, -ere, -trivi, -tritum. to drive forth; to trample, crush.
    leo, -onis, m. lion.
    uetulus (vetulus), -a, -um. little old, old.
    oleo, -ere, -ui. to smell.
    edentulus, -a, -um. toothless.
865 adsisto, -ere, adstiti. to stand.
    lora, -orum, n. pl. reins.
    stimulus, -i, m. goad.
    manust = manu est.
866 facitote: future imperative (pl.).
    sonitus, -us, m. noise, sound.
    ungula, -ae, f. hoof.
    appareo, -ere, -ui, -itum. to appear. Supply *ut* to introduce the sub-
        stantive clause after *facitote*: "bring it about that the sound
        of your hooves might appear."
867 inflecto, -ere, -exi, -exum. to bend, bow, curve.
    pernicitas, -atis, f. nimbleness, swiftness, agility. "in a swift
        course bring it about that the nimbleness of your feet be bent."

ME.II   *aside*

Haud male illanc hinc āmouī.

aloud, as if possessed

Nunc hunc impūrissumum,   853

barbātum, tremulum, Tīthōnum, quī cluet Cygnō patre--   854

threateningly

Ita mihi imperās, ut ego huius membra atque ossa atque artua   855

comminuam illō scīpiōne, quem ipse habet.

SE.   *defending himself with his cane*

Dabitur malum,   856

mē quidem sī attigeris aut sī propius ad mē accesseris.   857

ME.II   *as if addressing Apollo*

Faciam quod iubēs: securim capiam ancipitem atque hunc senem   858

osse fīnī dēdolābō assulātim uiscera.   859

SE.   *still flourishing his cane*

Enim uērō illud praecauendumst atque adcūrandumst mihi.   860

sānē ego illum metuō, ut minātur, nē quid male faxit mihi.   861

ME.II   *with another inspiration*

Multa mī imperās, Apollō: nunc equōs iunctōs iubēs   862

capere mē indomitōs, ferocīs, atque in currum inscendere,   863

pointing to SE.

ut ego hunc prōteram leōnem uetulum, olentem, ēdentulum.   864

pretending to mount a chariot

Iam adstitī in currum: iam lōra teneō, iam stimulum; in manūst.   865

agite, equī, facitōte sonitus ungulārum appāreat: 866

cursū celerī facite inflexa sit pedum pernīcitās.   867

868   mihin = mihine.

minor, -ari, -atus. to threaten + dat. minare = minaris.

denuo. (adv.). anew, again, once more.

869   impetus, -us, m. attack.

870   capillus, -i, m. hair.

currus, -us, m. chariot.

deripio, -ere, -ripui, -reptum. to pull down.

871   demuto, 1. to change, alter.

edictus, -i, m. proclamation, edict; order, command.

Apollo, -inis, m. the genitive is in apposition to *tuom*, which
      modifies both *imperium* and *edictum*.

872   eu. (interjection). alas!

morbus, -i, m. sickness, disease.

di = dei.

uostram (vestram). *morbum* and *fidem* are exclamatory accusatives.

873   uel hic: "even this man." The Senex points out Menaechmus as one
      example of a person afflicted by a "bitter and harsh illness"
      (872).

quam: how.

paulo. (adv.). a little.

874   ei. dative of *is*.

derepente. (adv.). suddenly, on a sudden.

incido, -ere, incidi. to fall upon + dat.

875   accerso, -ere. to summon.

medicus, -i, m. doctor.

quantum potest: "as quickly as possible."

876   conspectus, -us, m. sight.

877   ualens (valens): "although well."

878   quid. why.

cesso, 1. to delay.

saluos (salvus), -a, -om. safe. With *saluo* supply *mihi*, dat. after
      licet.

879-880 reuenio (revenio), -ire, -ueni, -uentum. to return.

881   platea, -ae, f. (Greek word). street.

aufugio, -ere, -fugi. to run away, flee.

SE.   *frightened*

Mihin equīs iunctīs mināre?

868

           ME.II   Ecce, Apollō, dēnuō

mē iubēs facere impetum in eum, quī stat, atque occīdere.

869

sed quis hic est, quī mē capillō hinc dē currū dēripit?

870

imperium tuom dēmūtat atque ēdictum Apollinis.

871

ME.II falls to the ground, apparently unconscious

SE.   *relieved*

DIALOGUE

Eu, morbum hercle acrem ac dūrum, dī, uostram fidem.

872

uel hic, quī insānit, quam ualuit paulō prius:

873

eī dērepentē tantus morbus incidit.

874

ībō atque accersam medicum iam quantum potest.

875

SE. exits to the spectators' right, to the forum.

ME.II   *peering cautiously around*

Iamne istī abiērunt, quaesō, ex conspectū meō,

876

quī mē uī cōgunt, ut ualens insāniam?

877

quid cessō abīre ad nāuem, dum saluō licet?

878

to the spectators

Vōs omnīs quaesō, sī senex reuēnerit,

879, 880

nē mē indicētis, quā plateā hinc aufūgerim.

881

ME.II exits to the spectators' left, to the harbor.

882 lumbus, -i, m. loin.
    sedeo, -ere, sedi, sessum. to sit.
883 recipio, -ere, -cepi, -ceptum. to take back. se recipere: to
    withdraw from some place or some thing.
884 odiosus, -a, -um. hateful, odious, disagreeable.
    tandem. (adv.). finally.
    aegrotus, -a, -um. ill, sick.
885 obligo, 1. to bind together, bind up. obligasse = obligauisse.
    crus, -uris, n. leg.
    Aesculapius, -ii, m. Greek god of healing.
886 bracchium, -ii, n. arm.
887 utrum...an. whether...or.
    faber, -bri, m. a workman, stone-cutter, carpenter.
888 incedo, -ere, -cessi, -cessum. to go or come along.
    formicinus, -a, -um. of or like ants. (formica, -ae, f. ant).
    gradus, -us, m. step, pace.
889 quid...morbi: partitive genitive: "what illness."
    esse illi: possessive dative.
    narro, 1. to tell.
890 laruatus (larvatus), -a, -um. bewitched, enchanted. (larua, -ae, f.
       ghost, spectre).
    cerritus, -a, -um. having a crazed brain, frantic, mad. (contraction
       of *cerebritus*). cerritust = cerritus est.
891 ueternus (veternus), -i, m. old age; lethargy, somnolence, torpidity.
    intercus, -cutis. under the skin (*cutis, -is*, f.). aqua intercus:
       "dropsy."
892 ea...causa: "for that reason."
893 perfacilis, -e. very easy.
    quidemst = quidem est.
894 mea...fide: "by my trust," "by my word."
    promitto, -ere, -misi, -missum. to promise.
896 suspiro, 1. to draw a deep breath, to sigh.
    plus. (adv.). more. (*quam* is omitted when the comparison is with
       numbers).
    sescenti, -ae, -a. six hundred. As noun, supply *suspiria*, "sighs"
       (cognate accusative). 600 was proverbial with the Romans of an
       immense number.
898 obseruo (observo), 1. to watch, observe.

889ff. Is this scene a burlesque of the fashionable doctor or is it a straight
       portrayal of an important professional? What is the status of the
       doctor in this period?

ACT VI

SE. enters slowly from spectators' right, from the forum.

SE.   Lumbī sedendō, oculī spectandō ᴊolent,   882

      manendō medicum, dum sē ex opere recipiat.   883

      odiōsus tandem uix ab aegrōtīs uenit.   884

      ait sē obligasse crūs fractum Aescᴜlāpiō,   885

      Apollinī autem bracchium: nunc cōgitō,   886

      utrum mē dīcam dūcere, medicum an fabrum.   897

looking back at the medicus who follows him onto the stage

      Atque eccum incēdit.

             to MED.

             Mouē formīcīnum gradum.   888

MED.   *pompously, to SE.*

      Quid esse illī morbī dīxerās? narrā, senex.   889

      num laruātus aut cerrītust? fac sciam.   890

      num eum ueternus aut aqua intercus tenet?   891

SE.   Quīn eā tē causā dūcō, ut id dīcās mihi   892

      atque illum ut sānum faciās.

                  MED. Perfacile id quidemst.   893

      sānum futūrum, meā ego id prōmittō fide.   894

SE.   Magnā cum cūrā ego illum cūrārī uolō.   895

MED. Quīn suspīrabō plūs sescentā in diē: 896

      ita ego eum cum cūrā magnā cūrābō tibi.   897

SE.   *looking down the street to the spectators' right and catching sight of ME.I, who enters, returning from the forum*

      Atque eccum ipsum hominem. obseruēmus, quam rem agat.   898

899 ne. (interjection). truly, really, indeed.
peruorsus (perversus), -a, -um. turned the wrong way, askew, awry.
aduorsus (adversus), -a, -um. turned against, opposite; adverse,
   unfavorable.
optingo, -ere, -tigi. to touch, strike; fall to one's lot + dat.
900 reor, reri, ratus. to reckon, calculate, think.
palam. (adv.). openly, publicly, plainly. palam facere: to reveal,
   make known.
901 compleo, -ere, -eui, -etum. to fill up someone with something (acc.
   and gen.).
flagitium, -ii, n. a shameful or disgraceful act or thing; shame,
   disgrace.
formido, -inis, f. fear, terror, dread.
902 Ulixes, -is, m. Ulysses, Odysseus. A name used proverbially of any
   clever person.
suo...regi: dative. rex: here of Menaechmus as the *patron* of his
   parasite, Peniculus.
tantum...mali. partitive genitive.
concieo, -ere, -ciui, -citum. to stir up, excite, produce, cause.
903 siquidem. (adv.). if indeed.
euoluo (evolvo), -ere, -uolui, -uolutum. to roll out, roll forth.
904 stultus, -a, -um. foolish, stupid.
illius: gen. "his." Menaechmus is speaking of Peniculus' life
   (*uita*).
905 sumptus, -us, m. expense, cost, outlay of money.
educo, 1. to bring up, rear. educatust = educatus est.
anima, -ae, f. air; the vital principle, breath of life; life. By
   anima, Menaechmus means the *cibus* and *sumptus* to which he has
   just referred.
priuo (privo), 1. to rob or strip someone (acc.) of something (abl.).
906 condigne. (adv.). very worthily.
meretricius, -a, -um. of or belonging to a *meretrix*.
907 rursum. (adv.). back, again.
908 eu. (interjection). oh! ah! alas!
ne. (interjection). truly, really, indeed.
uiuo (vivo) = sum.
909 audin = audisne.
praedico, 1. to say, state, declare.
adeas uelim: "I would like (that) you approach (him)."
910 saluos sis = salue. Greetings!
aperto, 1. to lay bare.
bracchium, -ii, n. arm.
911 quantum...mali: partitive genitive.
morbus, -i, m. sickness, illness.
912 suspendo, -ere, -di, -sum. to hang.
ecquis, ecquid. any one, any thing.
quidni. why...not? how...not?
sentiam: deliberative subjunctive.

ME.I   *to himself*

Edepol nē hic diēs peruorsus atque aduorsus mī obtigit: 899

quae mē clam ratus sum facere, omnia ea fēcit palam   900

parasītus, quī mē compleuit flāgitī et formīdinis,   901

meus Vlixēs, suō quī rēgī tantum conciuit malī: 902

quem ego hominem, sīquidem uiuō, uītā ēuoluam suā--   903

sed, ego stultus sum, quī illīus esse dīcō, quae meast: 904

meō cibō et sumptū ēducātust. animā priuabō uirum.   905

condignē autem haec meretrix fēcit, ut mōs est meretrīcius: 906

quia rogō, palla ut referātur rursum ad uxōrem meam,   907

mihi sē ait dedisse. eu edepol! nē ego homō uiuō miser.   908

SE.   *to MED.*

Audīn quae loquitur?

    MED.   Sē miserum praedicat.

        SE.   Adeās uelim.   909

MED.   *approaching ME.I, whose anger has caused his cloak to slip off his arm*

Saluos sīs, Menaechme. quaesō, cur apertās bracchium?   910

nōn tū scīs, quantum istī morbō nunc tuō faciās malī?   911

ME.I   *to MED.*

Quīn tū tē suspendis?

    SE.   *to MED.*

    Ecquid sentīs?

        MED.   *to SE.*

        Quidnī sentiam?   912

913   elleborus, -i, m. hellebore (a plant used by the ancients as a remedy
        for mental disease).
     iugerum, -i, n. an acre.
     obtineo, -ere, -tinui, -tentum. to hold, to get hold of, to control.
        obtinerier: passive infinitive.
915   albus, -a, -um. white.
     ater, -tra, -trum. black.
     uinum (vinum), -i, n. wine.
    *in malam crucem. see line 66.
916   occepto, 1. to begin.
     primulum. (dim. adv.). at first, first.
917   med = me.
    *interrogo, 1. to ask.
918   purpureus, -a, -um. purple.
     puniceus, -a, -um. red.
    *soleo, -ere, -itus. to be accustomed.
    *edo, edere *or* esse, edi, esum. to eat.
     luteus, -a, -um. saffron-yellow.
919   soleamne: "or whether I might be accustomed."
     auis (avis), -is, f. bird.
     squamosus, -a, -um. full of scales, scaly.
     piscis, -is, m. fish.
     pennatus, -a, -um. full of feathers, feathered.
     papae. (interjection). strange! indeed!
920   deliramentum, -i, n. nonsense, absurdity.
     cesso, 1. to cease from, stop. Quid cessas dare: "Why don't you
        give."
921   potio, -onis, f. a drink.
     percipio, -ere, -cepi, -ceptum. to seize entirely.
     insania, -ae, f. madness.
922   percontor, -ari, -atus. to ask, question.
     fabulor, -ari, -atus. to speak, talk.
924   locusta, -ae, f. lobster.
     ignauos (ignavus), -a, -om. inactive, lazy. here a general term of
        abuse: "good-for-nothing."

nōn potest haec rēs elleborī iūgerō obtinērier.   913

to ME.I

Sed quid ais, Menaechme?

        ME.I   Quid uīs?

                MED. Dīc mihi hoc quod tē rogō: 914

album an atrum uīnum pōtās?

             ME.I *annoyed*

                  Quīn tū īs in malam crucem?   915

MED. *to SE.*

Iam hercle occeptat insānīre prīmulum.

                  to ME.I

                Quīn tū mihi   916

id respondēs, quod rogāuī?

            ME.I Quīn tū mēd interrogās,   917

purpureum pānem an pūniceum soleam ego esse an lūteum?   918

soleamne esse auīs squāmōsās, piscīs pennātōs?

                  SE. *to MED.*

                    Papae,   919

audīn tū, ut dēlīrāmenta loquitur? quid cessās dare   920

pōtiōnis aliquid, prius quam percipit insānia?   921

MED. *to SE.*

Manē modo: etiam percontābor alia.

            SE. *to MED.*

                Occīdis fābulans.   922

MED. *to ME.I*

Dīc mihi hoc: solent tibi umquam oculī dūrī fīerī?   923

ME.I Quid? tū mē locustam censēs esse, homō ignāuissume?   924

925 enumquam. (adv.). ever.
   intestina, -orum, n. pl. guts, intestines.
   crepo, -are, -ui, -itum. to rattle, crack, creak; to make a noise.
926 satur, -ura, -urum. full of food.
   esurio, -ire, -itum. to be hungry.
927 pro insano: "as a madman."
   uerbum (verbum), -i, n. word.
928 perdormisco, -ere. to sleep on. perdormiscin = perdormiscine.
   lucem: "dawn."
   facile. (adv.). easily. facilen = facilene.
   dormio, -ire, -ii, -itum. to sleep.
   cubo, -are, -ui, -itum. to lie down.
929-930 resoluo (resolvo), -ere, -solui, -solutum. to untie, loosen; to pay.
   argentum, -i, n. silver; money.
   quoi = cui.
931-933 qui. (adv.). here with present subjunctive = utinam. I wish that,
   if only.
   percontator, -oris, m. an asker, inquirer.
   perduint: present subjunctive of *perdo, -ere, -didi, -ditum*, to
   destroy.
934 occepto, 1. to begin.
   *uerbum (verbum), -i, n. word.
   caueo (caveo), -ere, -caui, cautum. to be on one's guard, to watch
   out, beware.
935 Nestor, -oris, m. the wise counselor of the Greeks during the Trojan
   War.
   quidemst = quidem est.
   praeut. (adv.). in comparison with, compared with.
936 rabiosus, -a, -um. raving, mad, rabid.
   canis, -is, m. or f. dog.
937 insanu's = insanus es.
938 quadrigae, -arum, f. pl. a team of four horses; a chariot drawn by
   four horses.
   minitor, -ari, -atus. to threaten. minitatu's = minitatus es.
   prosterno, -ere, -straui, -stratum. to strew before one, to overthrow,
   prostrate.
939-940 egomet = ego.
   ted = te.
   arguo, -ere, -ui, -utum. to accuse, charge with.
941 sacer, sacra, sacrum. holy, sacred.
   *corona, -ae, f. wreath.
   Iuppiter, Iouis, m. the king of the gods.
942 carcer, -eris, m. prison.
   compingo, -ere, -pegi, -pactum. to put together; to confine, lock up.
943 emitto, -ere, -misi, -missus. to send or let out.
   caesum: "whipped." (from *caedo, -ere, cecidi, caesum*, to cut)
   uirga (virga), -ae, f. a twig, switch, rod.
   furca, -ae, f. a two-pronged fork; an instrument for punishment in
   the form of a fork placed on the culprit's neck.

MED. *to ME.I*

  Dīc mihi, ēnumquam intestīna tibi crepant, quod sentiās?   925

ME.I Vbi satur sum, nulla crepitant: quandō ēsuriō, tum crepant.   926

MED. *aside*

  Hoc quidem edepol haud prō insānō uerbum respondit mihi.   927

  to ME.I

  Perdormiscin usque ad lūcem? facilen tū dormīs cubans?   928

ME.I Perdormiscō, sī resoluī argentum, quoi dēbeō.   929, 930

  quī tē Iuppiter dīque omnēs, percontātor, perduint.   931, 933

MED. *to SE.*

  Nunc homō insānīre occeptat; dē illīs uerbīs cauē tibi.   934

SE. *to MED.*

  Immō Nestor nunc quidemst dē uerbīs, praeut dūdum fuit: 935

  nam dūdum uxōrem suam esse aiēbat rabiōsam canem.   936

ME.I *puzzled*

  Quid ego dīxī?

       SE. *to ME.I*

       Insānu's, inquam.

            ME.I Egone?

                 SE. *to ME.I*

                      tū istic, quī mihi   937

  etiam mē iunctīs quadrigīs minitātu's prosternere.   938

  egomet haec tē uīdī facere: egomet haec tēd arguō.   939, 940

ME.I *to SE.*

  At ego tē sacram corōnam surrupuisse Iouis scio   941

  et ob eam rem in carcerem tēd esse compactum scio: 942

  et postquam es ēmissus, caesum uirgīs sub furcā scio: 943

944 uendo (vendo), -ere, -didi, -ditum. to sell.
945 satin = satisne.
     pro sano: "like a sane man."
946 propere. (adv.). quickly.
     facturu's = facturus es.
     face = fac.
947 scin = scisne.
     optumumst = optumum est. "it is best."
948 uti = ut.
     quippini. why not?
949 arbitratus, -us, m. judgment, wish, choice; direction, guidance.
     lubet (libet), lubuit, lubitum. it pleases.
950 elleborus, -i, m. hellebore (a plant used by the ancients as a remedy
          for mental disease).
     aliqui, aliqua, aliquod. some. aliquos uiginti dies: "for about
          twenty days."
951 fodio, -ere, -fodi, fossum. to dig; to prick, pierce.
     stimulus, -i, m. a goad.
     triginta. thirty.
952 arcesso, -ere. to summon.
     quot. how many?
953 proinde ut. just as, according as, to the degree that.
     nihilo minus. no less.
954 adseruo (adservo), 1. to protect, guard.
955 ut parentur, quibus paratis opus est: "so that the things may be
          prepared for which there is need."
956 ego...faxo (= faciam). I'll see to it.
     illic = ille.
     uale (vale). farewell!

tum patrem occīdisse et mātrem uendidisse etiam sciō.   944

satin haec prō sānō male dicta male dictīs respondeō?   945

SE.   *to MED.*

Obsecrō hercle, medice, properē, quicquid factūru's, face.   946

nōn uidēs hominem insānīre?

                   MED.   *to SE.*

                        Scīn quid faciās optumumst?   947

ad mē face utī dēferātur.

                 SE.   Itane censēs?

                       MED.   Quippinī?   948

ibi meō arbitrātū poterō cūrāre hominem.

                    SE.   Age, ut lubet.   949

MED.   *to ME.I*

Elleborum pōtābis faxō aliquōs uīgintī diēs.   950

ME.I   *to MED.*

At ego tē pendentem fodiam stimulīs trīgintā diēs.   951

MED.   *to SE.*

Ī, arcesse hominēs, quī illunc ad mē dēferant.

                  SE.   Quot sunt satis?   952

MED.   Proinde ut insānīre uideō, quattuor, nihilō minus.   953

SE.   Iam hīc erunt. adseruā tū istunc, medice.

                MED.   Immō ibō domum,   954

ut parentur, quibus parātīs opus est. tū seruōs iube;   955

hunc ad mē ferant.

        SE.   Iam ego illīc faxō erit.

                 MED.   Abeō.

                   SE.   Valē.   956

957 socerus, -i, m. father-in-law.
    pro. (interjection). O! Ah!
958 hisce = hi.
    *praedico, 1. to say, state, declare.
959 *equidem. (adv.). truly, indeed.
    nascor, nasci, natus (gnatus). to be born.
    aegroto, 1. to be ill, sick.
960 pugna, -ae, f. a fist fight.
    lis, litis, f. strife, dispute, quarrel.
    coepio, coepi, coeptum (present tense very rarely used). to begin.
961 *saluos (salvus), -a, -om. saved, preserved, safe, well, sound.
    *adloquor, -i, -cutus. to speak to, address.
962 perperam. (adv.). wrongly, incorrectly, falsely.
963 sino, -ere, siui, situm. to allow.
964 intromitto, -ere, -misi, -missus. to send or let in.
    prouenio (provenio), -ire, -ueni, -uentum. to come forth; to arise,
       happen. prouentumst = prouentum est.
    nequiter. (adv.). worthlessly, badly.
965 saltem. (adv.). at least, anyhow.
966 spectamen, -inis, n. mark, sign, proof. "This is proof with respect
      to a good slave, one who..." = "This is proof of a good slave,
      who..."
    erilis, -e. of or belonging to a master, the master's.
967 procuro, 1. to take care of, attend to.
    conloco, 1. to place together, arrange, set in order.
968 absens, -entis. absent. absente ero: ablative absolute.
    erus, -i, m. master.
    diligenter. (adv.). carefully.
969 tutor, -ari, -atus. to watch, guard, protect.
    rectius. (comparative adv.). more rightly, better.
970 gula, -ae, f. gullet, throat.
    crus, -uris, n. leg.
    uenter (venter), -tris, m. belly.
971 potiora: "ought to be *more important* for him" (supply *ei*).
    quoi = cui.
    cor, cordis, n. heart.
    modeste. (adv.). moderately, discreetly, modestly.
    situs, -a, -um. placed, set. situmst = situm est.
972 recordor, -ari, -atus. to think over, be mindful of, remember.
      recordetur id: "let him remember this."
    nihili: gen. of value: "who are of no value, worthless."
    quid...preti: partitive genitive.
    pretium, -ii, n. money; worth; wages, reward.
    eis: i.e., qui nihili sunt.

966ff. How do Messenio's statements compare and contrast with those of
      Peniculus (77ff.)? How does each reflect his own status and the
      attitudes of his master or patron? Which of these underlings is more
      admirable? Why?

*MED. exits to spectators' right, to the forum, and SE. exits
warily into ME.I's house.*

ME.I   Abiit socerus, abiit medicus: sōlus sum. prō Iuppiter,   957

quid illuc est, quod mēd hīsce hominēs insānīre praedicant?   958

nam equidem, postquam gnātus sum, numquam aegrōtāuī ūnum diem.   959

neque ego insāniō neque pugnās neque ego lītīs coepiō.   960

saluos saluōs aliōs uideō, nōuī ego hominēs, adloquor.   961

an illī perperam insānīre mē aiunt, ipsī insāniunt?   962

quid ego nunc faciam? domum īre cupiō: uxor nōn sinit.   963

pointing to ER.'s house

Hūc autem nēmō intrōmittit: nimis prōuentumst nēquiter.   964

hīc erō usque: ad noctem saltem, crēdō, intrōmittar domum.   965

ME.I sits down at the door of his house.

*Messenio enters from spectators' left, from the harbor, looking
for his master. He does not see ME.I sitting in front of his
door.*

                                                                   SONG

MES.   Spectāmen bonō seruō id est, quī rem erīlem   966

procūrat, uidet, conlocat cōgitatque,   967

ut absente erō rem erī dīligenter   968

tūtētur, quam sī ipse adsit, aut rectius.   969

tergum quam gulam, crūra quam uentrem oportet   970

potiōra esse, quoi cor modestē situmst.   971

recordētur id, quī nihilī sunt, quid eīs pretī   972

973 ignauos (ignavus), -a, -om. lazy, idle.
    improbus, -a, -um. bad.
        972-973 "Let him remember this, what reward is given by their
        masters to those who are worthless, to idle, bad fellows."
974 uerber (verber), -eris, n. lash, whip, rod; lashing, flogging.
    compes, -edis, f. fetters, shackles (for the feet).
974a mola, -ae, f. millstone; mill.
    lassitudo, -inis, f. wariness, fatigue.
    frigus, -oris, n. cold.
975 pretium, -ii, n. reward.
    ignauia (ignavia), -ae, f. laziness, idleness.
976 metuo, -ere, -ui, -utum. to fear.
977 certumst = certum est. "it is fixed, certain." Supply *mihi* = "I have
        decided."
    potius quam. rather than.
978 facilius. (comparative adv.). more easily.
    uerba: i.e., of my master.
    uerber (verber), -eris, n. lash, whip, rod; lashing, scourging,
        flogging.
    odi, odisse. (perfect with present meaning). to hate.
979 nimio. (adv.). exceedingly, much, very. Modifies *lubentius*.
    lubentius (libentius). (comparative adv.). more willingly, cheer-
        fully, gladly.
    molitum, -i. bread (made from ground flour: *molo, -ere*, to grind).
    praehibeo, -ere. to offer, furnish, give, supply. molitum praehibere:
        to grind the flour.
980 erus, -i, m. master.
    exsequor, -i, -cutus. to follow up, perform, execute.
    sedate. (adv.). calmly.
981 prosum, prodesse, profui. to be useful to, to benefit, profit + dat.
982 ut in rem esse ducunt: "as they consider it to be to their advantage."
    ero: future of *sum*.
983 adhibeo, -ere, -ui, -itum. to bring to, to apply to. metum mihi
        adhibeam = "let me be fearful (or cautious)."
    culpa, -ae, f. fault, blame.
    abstineo, -ere, -ui, -tentum. to keep off or away, to hold at a dis-
        tance.
    ero: dative of *erus*.
    praesto. (adv.). at hand, ready, present. praesto esse: to be at
        hand, to attend, serve.
983a careo, -ere, -ui, -itum. to be without, be free from + abl.
    metuo, -ere, -ui, -utum. to fear.
    utibilis, -e. useful.
983b malum: "punishment."
    promereor, -eri, -itus. to deserve; to get. postquam malum
        promeriti (sunt): "after they have gotten their punishment."
984 metuam haud multum: "I won't fear much."
    prope quando: "(the time is) near when."
    facta: i.e., my "good deeds."
    pretium, -ii, n. reward.
    exsoluo (exsolvo), -ere, -solui, -solutum. to loose, set free; to pay.

detur ab suis eris, ignauis, improbis uiris.   973

verbera, compedes,   974

molae, lassitudo, fames, frigus durum: 974a

haec pretia sunt ignauiae.   975

id ego male malum metuo: 976

propterea bonum esse certumst potius quam malum.   977

nam magis multo patior facilius uerba, uerbera ego odi   978

nimioque edo lubentius molitum quam molitum praehibeo.   979

propterea eri imperium exsequor, bene et sedate seruo id: 980

atque id mihi prodest.   981

alii ita ut in rem esse ducunt, sint: ego ita ero ut me esse

oportet.   982

metum mihi adhibeam, culpam abstineam, ero ut omnibus in locis

sim praesto.   983

serui, qui, quom culpa carent, metuont, solent esse eris utibiles. 983a

nam illi qui nil metuont, postquam malum promeriti, tunc ei

metuont.   983b

metuam haud multum: prope quando erus ob facta pretium exsoluet.   984

985 exemplum, -i, n. example. eo...exemplo: "according to this example,"
    "in this way."
    in rem esse: "to be of advantage."
    arbitror, -ari, -atus. to think, suppose.
986 taberna, -ae, f. shop, tavern, inn.
    uasum (vasum), -i, n. vessel, dish; utensil, implement; baggage.
    conloco, 1. to place.
987 uenio aduorsum: "go to meet."
    pulto, 1. to strike, beat, knock.
988 saltus, -us, m. forest.
    damnum, -i, n. hurt, harm, damage, loss. ex hoc saltu damni: "from
    this den of iniquity."
    educo, -ere, -xi, -ctum. to lead out.
989 sero. (adv.). late; too late.
    depugno, 1. to fight to the end.
990 per: with *deos atque homines*.
991 sapienter. (adv.). wisely.
    curae: dative of purpose: "for a care."
992 medicina, -ae, f. doctor's office.
    ablatus...siet: "he be carried off."
    sublimis, -e. lifted up, borne aloft (on the shoulders).
993 *caueo (caveo), -ere, caui, cautum. to be on one's guard, to beware.
    caue quisquam...uostrum: "let anyone of you (= all of you)
    beware."
    minitor, -ari, -atus. to threaten.
    floccus, -i, m. a lock or flock of wool; something trifling, insig-
    nificant, of no account. flocci facere: to make no account of,
    to care not a straw for.
995 raptum: supply *esse*.
996 praesto. (adv.). at hand, ready, present. praesto esse: to be at
    hand, to attend, serve.
    occido, -ere, -cidi, -casum. to fall down; to perish, be ruined.
997 illisce: nom. pl.
998 quaerito, 1. to seek.
    circumsisto, -ere, -steti. to surround.

eō ego exemplō seruiō, tergō ut in rem esse arbitror.   985

Postquam in tabernam uāsa et seruōs conlōcāuī, ut iusserat,   986

ita ueniō aduorsum.

       going to the door of ER.'s house

       Nunc forīs pultābō, adesse ut mē sciat   987

atque uirum ex hōc saltū damnī saluom ut ēdūcam forās.   988

sed metuō nē sērō ueniam dēpugnātō proeliō.   989

SE. enters from ME.I's house accompanied by four strong slaves
*(*lorarii*).*

SE.   *to the* lorarii   RECITATIVE

Per ego uōbīs deōs atque hominēs dīcō, ut imperium meum   990

sapienter habeātis cūrae, quae imperāuī atque imperō.   991

pointing to ME.I

Facite illic homō iam in medicīnam ablātus sublīmis siet,   992

nisi quidem uōs uostra crūra aut latera nihilī penditis.   993

cauē quisquam, quod illic minitētur, uostrum floccī fēcerit.   994

quid stātis? quid dubitātis? iam sublīmem raptum oportuit.   995

ego ībō ad medicum: praestō erō illī, quom ueniētis.

SE. exits to the spectators' right, to the forum; the lorarii
rush at ME.I

                       ME.I Occidī.   996

quid hoc est negōtī? quid illīsce hominēs ad mē currunt, obsecrō? 997

quid uoltis uōs? quid quaeritātis? quid mē circumsistitis?   998

The lorarii *pick* ME.I *up and begin to carry him off.*

Quō rapitis mē? quō fertis mē? periī.

       calling for help

       Obsecrō uestram fidem,   999

1000   subuenio (subvenio), -ire, -ueni, -uentum. to come to one's assis-
        tance, to aid.
      mitto, -ere. to send; to let go.
1001   pro. (interjection). 0!
      immortalis, -e. immortal.
      aspicio, -ere, -spexi, -spectum. to see.
1002   indignissime. (superlative adv.). most unworthily, most shamefully.
      nescioqui = aliqui. "some people."
      sublimis, -e. lifted up, borne aloft.
1003   ecquis, ecquid. any one, any thing.
      suppetiae, -arum, f. pl. aid, assistance.
      *erus, -i, m. master.
      audacissime. (superlative adv.). most boldly.
1004   facinus, -oris, n. deed, act,
      indignus, -a, -um. unworthy, shameful.
1005   pacatus, -a, -um. peaceful.
      luci: locative. "in broad daylight."
      deripio, -ere, -ripui, -reptum. to snatch away. deripier: passive
         infinitive.
1008   neu. and that not.
      sino, -ere, -siui, situm. to allow, permit.
      insignite. (adv.). remarkably, notably.
1009   subuenio (subvenio), -ire, -ueni, -uentum. to come to one's assis-
        tance, to aid.
      sedulo. (adv.). diligently, eagerly.
1010   perirest = perire est.
      aequius est: "it is more fair."
1011   eripio, -ere, -ipui, -eptum. to pull out, snatch away.
      istic = isti (dat. of separation).
      umerus, -i, m. shoulder.
1012   hisce = his.
      sementis, -is, f. a seeding, sowing (here of blows from his fists).
      os, oris, n. mouth; face.
      pugnus, -i, m. fist.
      obsero, -ere, -seui, -situm. to sow, plant.
1013   maximo...malo uostro: ablative of attendant circumstance; "with the
        greatest ill on your part."
1014   huic: dative of reference.
      face = fac.
      appareo, -ere, -ui, -itum. to appear.

Epidamnienses, subuenīte, cīuēs.

to the lorarii

Quīn mē mittitis?   1000

MES.   *Suddenly catching sight of ME.I being carried off by the* lorarii

Prō dī immortālēs, obsecrō, quid ego oculīs aspiciō meīs?   1001

erum meum indignissimē nescīoquī sublīmem ferunt.   1002

ME.I   Ecquis suppetiās mī audet ferre?

MES.   *to ME.I*

Ego, ere audācissimē.   1003

ō facinus indignum et malum, Epidamniī cīuēs, erum   1004

meum hīc in pacātō oppidō lūcī dēripier in uiā,   1005

quī līber ad uōs uēnerit.   1006

to the lorarii

Mittite istunc.

ME.I   *to MES.*

Obsecrō tē, quisquis es, operam mihi ut dēs,   1007

neu sinās in mē insignītē fīerī tantam iniūriam.   1008

MES.   Immō et operam dabō et dēfendam et subuenībō sēdulō.   1009

numquam tē patiar perīre, mē perīrest aequius.   1010

ēripe oculum istīc, ab umerō quī tenet, ere, tē, obsecrō.   1011

hīsce ego iam sēmentem in ōre faciam pugnōsque obseram.   1012

to the lorarii

Maximō hercle hodiē malō uostrō istunc fertis: mittite.   1013

ME.I   *punching one* lorarius *in the eye*

Teneō ego huic oculum.

MES.   Face ut oculī locus in capite appāreat.   1014

1015   scelestus, -a, -um. wicked, villainous.
       raapx, -acis. rapacious.
       praedo, -onis, m. robber; pirate.
1016   tactio, -onis, f. a touching, touch. here with *me* as a direct object
          of the verbal idea in the noun. "Why are you touching me?"
          tactiost = tactio est.
1017   pecto, -ere, pexi, pexum. to comb.
1018   postremus, -a, -um. last.
       praemium, -ii, n. reward.
1019   os, oris, n. mouth, face.
       commeto, 1. to measure thoroughly. i.e., with his fists.
1020   ne. (interjection). surely, indeed.
       suppetiae, -arum, f. pl. aid, assistance. Here acc. after verb of
          motion: "I came to your aid."
       temperi. (adv.). on time.
1022   absque. (prep. with abl.). without. absque te esset: "had it
          been without you." esset...uiuerem: subjunctives in a contrary
          to fact condition.
       occido, -ere, -cidi, -casum. to fall down; (of heavenly bodies) to
          set.
1023   si...facias...emittas: future less vivid condition.
       emitto, -ere, -misi, -missus. to send forth; (with *manu*) to set free
          (of slaves).
1024   quandoquidem. (adv.). since indeed.

1020ff. What similar qualities of character are apparent in both brothers when
        they encounter friends and acquaintances of the other?

to the lorarii

Vōs scelestī, uōs rapācēs, uōs praedonēs.

LO. *getting the worst*
   of the fight

     Periimus.   1015

obsecrō hercle.

  MES. *to the* lorarii

    Mittite ergō.

     ME.I *to the* lorarii

       Quid mē uobīs tactiōst? 1016

to MES.

Pecte pugnīs.

  MES. *to the* lorarii

    Agite, abīte, fugite hinc in malam crucem. 1017

Lorarii *exit into ME.I's house. MES. kicks the last of the* lorarii *as he departs.*

Em tibi etiam: quia postrēmus cēdis, hoc praemī ferēs. 1018

nimis bene ōra commētauī atque ex meā sententiā. 1019

to ME.I

Edepol, ere, nē tibi suppetiās temperī aduenī modo. 1020

ME.I *to MES.*

At tibi dī semper, adulescens, quisquis es, faciant bene:: 1021

nam absque tē esset, hodiē numquam ad sōlem occāsum uiuerem. 1022

MES. Ergō edepol, sī rectē faciās, ere, mēd ēmittās manū. 1023

ME.I Līberem ego tē?

    MES. Vērum, quandōquidem, ere, tē seruauī.

       ME.I Quid est? 1024

1025   erro, 1. to wander; to make a mistake.
      Iuppiter, Iouis, m. the king and father of the gods.
      adiuro, 1. to swear.
1026 *med = me.
      taceo, -ere, cui, -citum. to be silent.
      mentior, -iri, -itus. to lie.
1027 nec...numquam: double negative for emphasis.
      tale...quale. such a thing as.
1028 sino, -ere, siui, situm. to permit, allow. Supply *me* with *abire*
         liberum.
1029 mea...causa: "as far as I am concerned."
      esto: future imperative of *sum.*
      ito: future imperative of *eo.*
1030 nempe. (adv.). indeed, certainly, really.
      si quid imperist in te mihi: "if I have any power over you."
         quid imperi: partitive gen. *mihi* is possessive dative.
         imperist = imperi est.
1031 *salue (salve). (imperative). Health! Greetings!
1032 gaudeo, -ere, gauisus. to be glad.
      patronus, -i, m. patron.
1033 minus. (adv.). less.
1034 ted = te.
      habito, 1. to live.
1035 minime. (adv.). least of all, not at all, no.
      taberna, -ae, f. shop, tavern, inn.
      uasum (vasum), -i, n. dish, utensil, implement; baggage.
      argentum, -i, n. silver money.
1036 *recte. (adv.). rightly, properly. rectest = recte est.
      obsigno, 1. to seal (a will, letter, package, etc.).
      uidulus (vidulus), -i, m. travelling-trunk, luggage.
      marsuppium, -ii, n. purse.
1037 uiaticum (viaticum), -i, n. travelling-money.
      strenue. (adv.). briskly, quickly, promptly.
1038 reddibo: future in -*ibo* from *reddo, -ere.*

adulescens, errās.

        MES. Quid, errō?

                ME.I Per Iouem adiūrō patrem   1025

mēd erum tuom nōn esse.

        MES. Nōn tacēs?

                ME.I Nōn mentior: 1026

nec meus seruos numquam tāle fēcit quāle tū mihi.   1027

MES. Sīc sine igitur, sī tuom negās mē esse, abīre līberum.   1028

ME.I Meā quidem hercle causā līber estō atque ītō quō uolēs.   1029

MES. Nemp' iubēs?

        ME.I Iubeō hercle, sī quid imperīst in tē mihi.   1030

MES. Saluē, mī patrōne. 'quom tū līber es, Messēniō,   1031

gaudeō'.

      to the spectators

      Crēdō hercle uōbīs.

          to ME.I

                Sed, patrōne, tē obsecrō,   1032

nē minus imperēs mihi, quam quom tuos seruos fuī.   1033

apud tēd habitābō et, quandō ībis, ūnā tēcum ībō domum.   1034

ME.I *aside*

Minimē.

        MES. Nunc ībō in tabernam, uāsa atque argentum tibi   1035

referam. rectēst obsignātum in uidulō marsuppium   1036

cum uiāticō: id tibi iam hūc adferam.

                ME.I Adfer strēnuē.   1037

MES. Saluom tibi ita, ut mihi dedistī, reddībō. hīc mē manē.   1038

MES. exits to the spectators' left, to the harbor.

1039   nimius, -a, -um. beyond measure, excessive, too great, too much.
      mirus, -a, -um. wonderful, marvelous, extraordinary.
      exorior, -iri, -ortus. to come forth, spring up (suddenly and unex-
          pectedly).
1040   excludo, -ere, -si, -sum. to shut out.
1041   emisi manu: cf. 1023.
1042   Line lost from the manuscripts.
1043   *affero, afferre, attuli, allatum. to bring. allaturum: future active
          participle.
1046   socer, -eri, m. father-in-law.
1047   nihilum, -i, n. nothing. nihilo (with comparative): by nothing, no.
      secus. (adv.). otherwise, differently. Comparative: setius; same
          meaning. nihilo...setius: no differently, no less, just as.
      somnium, -ii, n. dream.
1048   quamquam. (conj.). although.
      suscenseo, -ere, -sui, -sum. to be angry.
1049   exoro, 1. to move, prevail upon, persuade.

ME.I   *alone and bewildered*

Nimia mīra mihi quidem hodiē exorta sunt mīrīs modīs.   1039

aliī mē negant eum esse quī sum atque exclūdunt forās,   1040

etiam hic seruom sē meum esse aibat quem ego ēmīsī manū.   1041

. . . .   1042

is ait sē mihi allātūrum cum argentō marsuppium.   1043

id sī attulerit, dīcam ut ā mē abeat līber quō uolet,   1044

nē tum, quandō sānus factus sit, ā mē argentum petat.   1045

socer et medicus mē insānīre aiēbant. quid sit, mīra sunt.   1046

haec nihilō esse mihi uidentur sētius quam somnia.   1047

nunc ībō intrō ad hanc meretrīcem, quamquam suscenset mihi,   1048

sī possum exōrāre, ut pallam reddat, quam referam domum.   1049

ME.I exits into ER.'s house.

1050   men = mene.
      *usquam. (adv.). ever.
      conuenio (convenio), -ire, -ueni, -uentum. to meet.
1051   aduorsum...uenire: to come to meet.
1052   eripio, -ere, -ipui, -eptum. to snatch away.
      sublimis, -e. raised up, aloft.
1053   deum = deorum.
1054   accurro, -ere, accurri, accursum. to run to.
      pugno, 1. to fight.
      ingratiis. (adv.). unwillingly, against their will.
1055   amitto, -ere, -misi, -missum. to send away, to let go.
1056   *argentum, -i, n. silver; money.
1057   praecurro, -ere, -cucurri, -cursum. to run before, to hasten on
        before.
      obuiam (obviam). (adv.). in the way, towards, against, to meet.
      infitiae, -arum, f. pl. denial. infitias ire: to deny.
1058   certissimumst = certissimum est.
1059   mepte = me.
1060   ea causa: "for that reason."
1061   pessumus (pessimus), -a, -um. worst.
1062 *pro. (interjection). O!
      speculum, -i, n. mirror.
1063   negotist = negoti est.
      imago, -inis, f. imitation, copy, image, likeness.
      consimilis, -e. similar in all respects.
1064   profecto. (adv.). actually, indeed, really, truly.
      dissimilis, -e. dissimilar.
      noscito, 1. to know, recognize; to perceive, observe.

1060ff. What is the purpose of this elongated recognition scene? Since the
truth is always known to the audience, why does Plautus picture the
twins as so slow to comprehend the truth? Does the scene support the
contention that the most entertaining character for Plautus and his
audience is the slave with his cleverness and superiority to his master and his ultimate reward? Or should we see here some deeper signif-
icance in an individual slowly facing the reality of himself and
becoming fully adjusted?

ACT VII

ME.II and MES. enter together from spectators' left, from the harbor.

ME.II   *to MES.*

Mēn hodiē usquam conuēnisse tē, audax, audēs dīcere,   1050

postquam aduorsum mī imperāuī ut hūc uenīrēs?

                          MES.   Quīn modo   1051

ēripuī hominēs quī ferēbant tē sublīmem quattuor,   1052

apud hāsce aedīs. tū clamābās deum fidem atque hominum omnium,   1053

quom ego accurrō tēque ēripiō uī pugnandō ingrātiīs.   1054

ob eam rem, quia tē seruāuī, mē āmīsistī līberum.   1055

quom argentum dīxī mē petere et uāsa, tū quantum potest   1056

praecucurristī obuiam ut, quae fēcistī, infitiās eās.   1057

ME.II   Līberum ego tē iussī abīre?

               MES.   Certō.

                     ME.II   Quīn certissimumst   1058

mēpte potius fīerī seruom, quam tē umquam ēmittam manū.   1059

ME.I enters from ER.'s house, speaking to those within

ME.I   Sī uoltis per oculōs iūrāre, nihilō hercle eā causā magis   1060

faciētis ut ego hinc hodiē abstulerim pallam et spintēr, pessumae.   1061

MES.   *amazed, as he catches sight of ME.I*

Prō dī immortālēs, quid ego uideō?

                  ME.II   Quid uidēs?

                     MES.   Speculum tuom.   1062

ME.II   Quid negōtīst?

             MES.   Tuast imāgō: tam consimilest quam potest.   1063

ME.II   *staring at ME.I*

Pol profectō haud est dissimilis, meam quom formam noscitō.   1064

1066   eloquor, -i, -locutus. to speak out, tell. eloquere: imperative.
       piget, piguit, pigitum est. it irks, troubles, displeases (supply *te*).
1067   promereo, -ere, -ui, -itum. to deserve, merit.
1068   obsequor, -i, -cutus. to comply with, yield to.
       mihist = mihi est.
1069   patria, -ae, f. fatherland. patriast = patria est.
1071   med = me.
1072   exhibeo, -ere, -ui, -itum. to hold forth, present, produce.
          exhibui negotium: "I gave him trouble."
1073   ignosco, -ere, -noui, -notum. to pardon, forgive, excuse.
       quid = aliquid.
    *stulte. (adv.). foolishly.
       imprudens, -entis. without knowing, unaware, inconsiderate.
1074   deliro, 1. to be crazy, to rave.
       uidere = uideris. "you seem."
       commemini, -isse. to remember.
1075 *exeo, -ire, -ii, -itum. to go out.
       enim uero. yes indeed, certainly.
       aequom postulas: "you make a reasonable demand."

ME.I   *to MES.*

Ō adulescens, saluē, quī mē seruāuistī, quisquis es.   1065

MES.   *to ME.I*

Adulescens, quaesō hercle, ēloquere tuom mihi nōmen, nisi piget.   1066

ME.I   Nōn edepol ita prōmeruistī dē mē, ut pigeat quae uelīs   1067

obsequī. mihist Menaechmō nōmen.

                         ME.II   Immō edepol mihi.   1068

ME.I   Siculus sum Syrācusānus.

                     ME.II   Ea domus et patriast mihi.   1069

ME.I   Quid ego ex tē audiō?

        ME.II   Hoc quod rēs est.

             MES.   *to ME.I*

                  Nōuī equidem hunc: erus est meus.   1070

ego quidem huius seruos sum.

                    nodding at ME.II

                  Sed mēd esse huius crēdidī.   1071

pointing first to ME.II, then to ME.I

Ego hunc censēbam tēd esse.

                  pointing to ME.II

                  Huic etiam exhibuī negōtium.   1072

to ME.II

Quaesō ignoscās, sī quid stultē dīxī atque imprūdens tibi.   1073

ME.II   Dēlīrāre mihi uidēre. nōn commeministī simul   1074

tē hodiē mēcum exīre ex nāuī?

             MES.   Enim uērō aequom postulās.   1075

1076   salueto: future imperative. "Greetings!"
      uale (vale). "Farewell."
1077   fabula, -ae, f. story. fabulast = fabula est.
1078   tu's = tu es.
      prognatus, -a, -um. born from.
1079   tun = tune.
      patre's = patre es.
1080   praeripio, -ere, -ripui, -reptum. to snatch away, carry off.
1081   insperatus, -a, -um. unhoped for.
1082 *gemini, -ae, -a. twin.
    *germanus, -i, m. brother.
1083   commemoro, 1. to remember; to mention.
      pariter. (adv.). equally.
1084   seuoco (sevoco), 1. to call apart or aside.
      ambo, ambae, ambo. both.
1085   uostrorumst = uostrorum est. uostrorum = vestrum.
      adueho (adveho), -ere, -xi, -ctum. to carry, bring; (passive) to be
         carried, to ride, to come to a place.

to ME.II

Tū erus es.

    to ME.I

    Tu seruom quaere.

        to ME.II

        Tū saluētō.

            to ME.I

            Tū ualē.　　　　　　　1076

pointing to ME.II

Hunc ego esse āiō Menaechmum.

        ME.I　At ego mē.

          ME.II　Quae haec fābulast?　　1077

tū's Menaechmus?

      ME.I　Mē esse dīcō, Moschō prōgnātum patre.　　1078

ME.II　Tūn meō patre's prōgnātus?

        ME.I　Immō equidem, adulescens, meō.　　1079

tuom tibi neque occupāre neque praeripere postulō.　　1080

MES.　Dī immortālēs, spem insperātam date mihi, quam suspicor.　　1081

nam nisi mē animus fallit, hī sunt geminī germānī duo:　　1082

nam et patrem et patriam commemorant pariter quae fuerint sibi.　　1083

sēuocābō erum. Menaechme.

      ME.I and II　*both answering together*

      Quid uīs?

        MES.　Nōn ambōs uolō,　　1084

sed uter uostrōrumst aduectus mēcum nāuī.

        ME.I　Nōn ego.　　1085

1086 huc concede: "come over here."
1087 sycophanta, -ae, m. (Greek word). an informer; a trickster, cheat.
1088 similior, -ius: comparative of *similis*. Followed by genitive: "more
       similar to."
     alterum = alium.
1089 lacte, lactis, n. milk.
1090 tuist = tui est.
     tui: gen. of *tu*.
     post. (adv.). after; in addition.
1091 memoro, 1. to remember; to mention.
     meliust = melius est: "it is better."
     percontor, -ari, -atus. to question. percontarier: passive
       infinitive.
1092 qui. (adv.). how.
     admoneo, -ere, -ui, -itum. to remind, warn.
1093 pergo, -ere, perrexi, perrectum. to continue, go on, proceed.
     esto: future imperative of *sum*.
1094 fore = futurum esse (future infinitive of *sum*).
1095 opinor, -ari, -atus. to believe, think.
1097 natust = natus est.
1098 dixti = dixisti.
     itidem. (adv.). in like manner, just so.
1099 operam...dare: to give attention to.
     *ambo, -ae, -o. both.
1100 promereo, -ere, -ui, -itum. to deserve, merit.
     quid = aliquid. "you have deserved that you should not ask for any-
       thing but that you should get what you wish (*quod uelis*).
1101 tam quasi: "just as if."
     me emeris argento: "you had bought me with money."
     seruibo = seruiam (fut. ind.).

ME.II   At ego.

    MES.   *to ME.II*

        Tē uolō igitur.   hūc concēde.

             ME.II   *obeying*

                  Concessī.   quid est?   1086

to ME.II privately

MES.   Illic homō aut sycophanta aut geminus est frāter tuos.   1087

nam ego hominem hominis similiōrem nunquam uīdī alterum,   1088

neque aqua aquae nec lacte est lactis, crēde mī, usquam similius   1089

quam hīc tuīst tūque huius autem; post eandem patriam ac patrem   1090

memorat. meliust nōs adīre atque hunc percontārier.   1091

ME.II   *to MES.*

Hercle quī tū mē admonuistī rectē et habeō grātiam.   1092

perge operam dare, obsecrō hercle: līber estō, sī inuenīs   1093

hunc meum frātrem esse.

            MES.   Spērō

               ME.II   Et ego idem spērō fore.   1094

MES.   *to ME.I*

Quid ais tū? Menaechmum, opīnor, tē uocārī dīxerās.   1095

ME.I   Ita uerō.

        MES.   Huic item Menaechmō nōmen est. in Siciliā   1096

tē Syrācusīs nātum esse dīxistī: hīc nātust ibi.   1097

Moschum tibi patrem fuisse dīxtī: huic itidem fuit.   1098

nunc operam potestis ambo et mihi dare et uobīs simul.   1099

ME.I   *to MES.*

Prōmeruistī ut nē quid ōrēs, quod uelīs quīn impetrēs.   1100

tam quasi mē ēmeris argentō, līber seruībō tibi.   1101

1102   inuenturum: supply *me*; "that I will find you..."
1104   mirus, -a, -um. wonderful, marvelous, extraordinary.
        memoro, 1. to remember; to mention.
        utinam. I wish that! if only! + subjunctive.
        possies = possis.
1105   agite: "come now!"
1106   ubi. (adv.). when.
        lubet (libet), lubuit, lubitum est. it pleases.
        reticeo, -ere, -cui. to be silent, keep silence.
1107   fateor, -eri, fassus. to admit, grant, acknowledge.
        itidem. (adv.). in like manner, so, just, in the same way.
1109   quippini. why not? = certainly, to be sure, by all means.
1110   optime. (superlative adv.). best.
        adhuc. (adv.). to this place, thus far.
        conuenio (convenio), -ire, -ueni, -uentum. to come together, to fit
            together.
        porro. (adv.). forward, onward; again, in turn.
1111   memini, -isse. to remember.
1112   mercatus, -us, m. market-place, market.
1113   deerro, 1. to wander away from.
        aueho (aveho), -ere, -uexi, -uectum. to carry off.

MES Spēs mihist uōs inuentūrum frātrēs germānōs duōs   1102

    geminōs, ūnā mātre nātōs et patre ūnō ūnō diē.   1103

ME.I Mīra memorās. utinam efficere, quod pollicitu's, possiēs. 1104

MES. Possum. sed nunc agite, uterque id, quod rogābō, dīcite. 1105

ME.I Vbi lubet, rogā: respondēbō, nīl reticēbō quod sciam. 1106

MES. *to ME.I*

    Est tibi nōmen Menaechmō?

       ME.I Fateor.

        MES. *to ME.II*

          Est itidem tibi?   1107

ME.II Est.

   MES. *to ME.I*

    Patrem fuisse Moschum tibi ais?

       ME.I Ita uērō.

        ME.II Et mihi.   1108

MES. *to ME.I*

    Esne tū Syrācusānus?

      ME.I Certō.

        MES. *to ME.II*

         Quid tū?

        ME.II Quippinī?   1109

MES. Optimē usque adhūc conueniunt signa. porrō operam date. 1110

    to ME.I

    Quid longissimē meministī, dīc mihi, in patriā tuā? 1111

ME.I Cum patre ut abiī Tarentum ad mercātum, posteā   1112

    inter hominēs mē dēerrāre ā patre atque inde āuehī. 1113

1114   supremus, -a, -um. highest.
1115   gnatus = natus. quot eras annos gnatus: "How old were you?"
1116   septuennis, -e. seven years old.
       dens, -entis, m. tooth.
       primulum. (adv.). at first, first.
1117   postilla. (adv.). after that.
       patri: dative of reference.
1118   maxime. (superlative adv.). especially.
1119   tun = tune.
       maior. bigger; older.
1120   qui. how.
1121   interpello, 1. to interrupt.
       potius. (adv.). rather.
1122   minime. (superlative adv.). least of all; no.
1124   adgnosco, -ere, -noui, nitum. to recognize.
       contineri: "to restrain myself."
       complector, -i, -plexus. to embrace.
       queo, -ire, -ii, -itum. to be able.

ME.II   *exclaiming*

      Iuppiter suprēme, seruā mē.

                  MES. *crossly to ME.II*

                          Quid clāmās? quīn tacēs?   1114

to ME.I

Quot erās annōs gnatus quom tē pater ā patriā āuehit?   1115

ME.I   Septuennis: nam tunc dentēs mihi cadēbant prīmulum.   1116

neque patrem numquam postillā uīdī.

                      MES. Quid? uōs tum patrī   1117

fīliī quot erātis?

                  ME.I Vt nunc maximē meminī, duo.   1118

MES.   Vter erātis, tūn an ille, maior?

                  ME.I Aequē ambo parēs.   1119

MES.   Quī id potest?

        ME.I Geminī ambo erāmus.

                ME.II *exclaiming*

                    Dī mē seruātum uolunt.   1120

severely to ME.II

MES.   Sī interpellās, ego tacēbō.

           ME.II Potius taceō.

                MES. *to ME.I*

                    Dīc mihi: 1121

unō nōmine ambo erātis?

              ME.I Minimē: nam mihi hoc erat,   1122

quod nunc est, Menaechmō: illum tum uocābant Sōsiclem.   1123

ME.II Signa adgnōuī: continērī quīn complectar nōn queō.   1124

mī germāne gemine frāter, saluē: ego sum Sōsiclēs.   1125

1127   renuntio, 1. to announce. renuntiatumst = renuntiatum est.
       deerro, 1. to wander from.
1128   ignotus, -a, -um. unknown.
       mortuos (mortuus), -a, -om. dead.
1129   auos (avus), -i, m. grandfather.
1131   conuenio (convenio), -ire, -ueni, -uentum. to come together, to fit
       together.
1132   insperatus, -a, -um. unhoped for.
1133   miseria, -ae, f. wretchedness, misery, distress.
1134   adhuc. (adv.). to this place, thus far.
   *gaudeo, -ere, gauisus. to be glad.
1135   hoc erat, quod: "this was the reason why."
1137   apparo, 1. to prepare. appararier: present passive infinitive.
1139   east = ea est.
1140   peruenio, -ire, -ueni, -uentum. to come to, to fall to.
1141   abduco, -ere, -xi, -ctum. to lead away.
       prandeo, -ere, -di, -sum. to eat lunch.
       perbene. (adv.). very well.
1142   accumbo, -ere, -cubui, -cubitum. to lay one's self down; to recline
       at table; to lie with (a woman).
       scortum, -i, n. courtesan.
1143   quid = aliquid (with *boni* as partitive genitive).
       euenio (evenio), -ire, -ueni, -uentum. to come forth; to come to
       pass, happen.

ME.I   *hesitating*

     Quō modo igitur post Menaechmō nōmen est factum tibi?   1126

ME.II Postquam ad nōs renuntiātumst tē dēerrasse ā patre   1127

     et surruptum ab homine ignōtō et patrem esse mortuom,   1128

     auos noster mutāuit: quod tibi nōmen est, fēcit mihi.   1129

ME.I   Credō ita esse factum ut dīcis. sed mī hoc respondē.

                                 ME.II Rogā.   1130

ME.I   Quid erat nōmen nostrae mātrī?

               ME.II Teuximarchae.

                          ME.I Conuenit.   1131

     ō saluē, insperāte, multīs annīs post quem conspicor.   1132

ME.II Frāter, et tū, quem ego multīs miseriīs, labōribus   1133

     usque adhūc quaesīuī quemque ego esse inuentum gaudeō.   1134

MES.   *to ME.II*

     Hoc erat, quod haec tē meretrix huius uocābat nōmine: 1135

     hunc censēbat tē esse, crēdō, quom uocat tē ad prandium.   1136

ME.I   Namque edepol iussī hīc mihi hodiē prandium appārārier   1137

     clam meam uxōrem, quoi pallam surrupuī dūdum domō: 1138

     eam dedī huic.

         ME.II *showing the* palla

               Hanc dīcis, frāter, pallam, quam ego habeō?

                      ME.I Haec east.   1139

     quō modō haec ad tē peruēnit?

                   ME.I Meretrix hūc ad prandium   1140

     mē abdūxit; mē sibi dedisse aiēbat. prandī perbene,   1141

     potāuī atque accubuī scortum: pallam et aurum hoc abstulī.   1142

ME.I   Gaudeō edepol, sī quid propter mē tibi euēnit bonī: 1143

1144-1145 memet = me.
 1146 numquid. (interrogative adv.). This word simply signals a question
    and need not be translated.
   morare = moraris; 2nd person singular of *moror*, to delay.
   iusti = iussisti.
   siem = sim.
 1147 optumus (optimus), -a, -um. best.
   causa mea: "for my sake."
 1148 esto. future imperative of *sum*.
   tu's = tu es.
1149-1150 meliorest = meliore est.
   melior, melius. better.
   opus (est). there is need for + abl.
   auspicium, -ii, n. a sign, omen, token. (i.e., a gift of money).
   perpetuo. (adv.). continually.
 1151 euenio (evenio), -ire, -ueni, -uentum. to come out, happen.
    euenere = euenerunt.
 1153 auctio, -onis, f. a public sale, auction.
   uendo (vendo), -ere, -didi, -ditum. to sell.
   quidquid = quicquid. whatever. quidquid est (supply *mihi*): "whatever
    I have."
 1154 scitin = scitisne.
 1155 praeconium, -ii, n. the office of a public crier or auctioneer.
   nunciam. (adv.). now.
 1156 conclamo, 1. to proclaim.
   fore = futuram esse. "that it will be."
   die septimi: locative. "on the seventh day."
 1157 mane. (adv.). in the morning.
   sane. (adv.). certainly, to be sure, indeed.
 1158 ueneo (veneo), -ire, -ii, -itum. to be sold.
   supellex, -lectilis, f. furniture, goods.
   fundus, -i, m. farm, estate.
 1159 quiqui = quoquo: ablative of price. "for whatever."
   liceo, -ere, -cui, -citum. to be valued. quiqui licebunt: "for
    whatever they will bring."
   praesenti pecunia: "for cash."
 1160 emptor, -oris, m. buyer.

nam illa quom tē ad sē uocābat, mēmet esse crēdidit.   1144, 1145

MES.   *to ME.I*

Numquid me morāre, quīn ego līber, ut iustī, siem?   1146

ME.I   Optumum atque aequissumum ōrat, frāter: fac causā meā.   1147

ME.II   Līber estō.

       ME.I   Quom tū's līber, gaudeō, Messēniō.   1148

MES.   Sed meliōrest opus auspiciō, ut līber perpetuō siem.   1149, 1150

ME.II   *ignoring MES.'s plea, and moving toward the house*

Quoniam haec ēuēnēre, frāter, nostrā ex sententiā,   1151

in patriam redeāmus ambo.

       ME.I   Frāter, faciam ut tū uolēs.   1152

auctiōnem hīc faciam et uendam quidquid est. nunc interim   1153

eāmus intrō, frāter.

       ME.II   Fīat.

       MES.   Scītin quid ego uōs rogō?   1154

ME.I   Quid?

   MES.   Praecōnium mī ut dētis.

      ME.I   Dabitur.

       MES.   Ergō nunciam   1155

vīs conclāmārī auctiōnem?

       ME.I   Fore quidem diē septimī.   1156

The brothers exit into ME.I's house

MES.   *to spectators*

Auctiō fiet Menaechmī māne sānē septimī.   1157

uēnībunt seruī, supellex, fundī, aedēs; omnia   1158

uēnībunt, quīquī licēbunt, praesentī pecūniā.   1159

uēnībunt uxor quoque etiam, sī quis emptor uēnerit.   1160

1161 quinquagesies. (adv.). fifty times. centena milia sestertium, "a
     hundred thousand sesterces," is understood along with
     quinquagesies = 5,000,000 sesterces: a *very* large sum of
     money.
1162 spectator, -oris, m. spectator.
     ualete (valete): "farewell."
     clare. (adv.). clearly.
     plaudo, -ere, -si, -sum. to clap.

Two important and recurring motifs of the play are bondage (e.g., to
food, to marriage, to responsibilities of citizenship, to the search
for a lost family member, to a master, etc.) and madness. How has
Plautus used them throughout and made them an integral part of the
plot? How are they interrelated? Which is the most important for the
theme of the play? Which adds the most to the humor?

uix crēdō auctiōne tōtā capiet quinquāgēsiēs.   1161

Nunc, spectātōrēs, ualēte et nōbīs clārē plaudite.   1162

                                                                Exit.

VOCABULARY

ab, a, (prep. w. abl.). from, away from; by.
*abeo, -ire, -ii, -itum. to go away, depart.
accedo, -ere, -cessi, -um. go toward; approach; be added.
accipio, -ere, -cepi, acceptum. receive; accept.
acer, acris, acre. sharp; keen; eager.
ad. (prep. w. acc.). to, toward; near.
adeo. (adv.). so, to such a degree; in addition.
*adeo, -ire, -ii, -itum. to go to, approach
adgredior, -i, -gressum. approach; attack.
*adloquor, -i, -cutus. to speak to, address.
adsum, -esse, -fui, -futurum. be present.
adulescens, -entis, m. young man.
*advenio, -ire, -i, -ventum. to come.
*aedes, -is, f. (often in pl. with singular sense). house.
aegre. (adv.). feebly; with difficulty.
aequus, -a, -um. level; favorable; equal; fair, reasonable.
aetas, -atis, f. age, time of life.
*affero, afferre, attuli, allatum. to bring.
ago, agere, egi, actum. do, act; drive; treat.
aio, ais, ait, aiunt. to say; to say yes, to affirm.
alienus, -a, -um. foreign; unfavorable.
aliquis, aliquid. someone, anyone; anything.
aliter. (adv.). otherwise.
alius, -a, -ud. other, another.
alo, -ere, alui, alitum or altum. feed; nourish; support.
alter, -a, -um. the one or the other (of two).
altus, -a, -um. high; deep.
*ambo, -ae, -o. both.
*ambulo, 1. to walk.
amicus, -i, m. friend.
amitto, -ere, -misi, missum. lose; send away.
amplius. (adv.). more, more than.
an. (conj.). or.
animus, -i, m. mind; courage.
annus, -i, m. year.
ante (prep. w. acc.). before.
aperio, -ire, -ui, apertum. open.
appello, 1. name, call; address.
apud. (prep. w. acc.). in the presence of; among; with; at the house of.
aqua, -ae, f. water.
aquila, -ae, f. eagle.
arbitror, 1. think.
arbor, -oris, f. tree.
arcesso, -ere, -ivi, -itum. summon, invite.
*argentum, -i, n. silver; money.
at. (conj.). but.
atque, ac. (conj.). and.
attingo, -ere, attigi, -tactum. touch; reach.
audax, -acis. bold, daring.
*audeo, -ere, ausus. to have a mind to do something, to be prepared, to
    intend; to dare.

audio, -ire, -ii, -itum. hear; obey + dat.
*aufero, auferre, abstuli, ablatum. to take away.
augeo, -ere, auxi, auctum. increase.
*aurum, -i, n. gold.
aut. (conj.). or.
aut...aut. either...or.
autem. (conj.). moreover.

bene. (adv.). well.
bis. (adv.). twice.
bonus, -a, -um. good.

cado, -ere, cecidi, casum. fall.
caedo, -ere, cecidi, caesum. cut down; kill.
capio, -ere, cepi, captum. take, capture.
captivus, -i, m. captive.
caput, -itis, n. head.
causa, -ae, f. cause, reason, case (at law).
causa (w. gen.). for the sake of.
*caveo, -ere, cavi, cautum. to be on one's guard, to beware.
cedo, -ere, cessi, cessum. go, go away; give way, yield.
celer, -eris, -ere. swift.
censeo, -ere, -ui, censum. estimate; think; decide; vote.
*certo. (adv.). certainly.
certus, -a, -um. fixed; certain; sure.
ceteri, -ae, -a. (pl.). the rest of, the other.
cibus, -i, m. food.
civis, -is, m. citizen.
clam. (adv.). secretly; without the knowledge of, in secret from + acc.
clamo, 1. shout.
*clanculum. (adv.). secretly.
cliens, -entis, m. client; follower.
coepi, -isse, coeptum. have begun, began.
cogito, 1. plan, think over, consider.
cognosco, -ere, -novi, cognitum. learn; (perf.) know.
cogo, -ere, coegi, coactum. collect; compel.
concedo, -ere, -cessi, -cessum. yield, grant, concede, withdraw.
conficio, -ere, -feci, -fectum. accomplish, finish.
consilium, -ii, n. plan, counsel.
conspicio, -ere, -spexi, -spectum. see, catch sight of.
conspicor, 1. catch sight of.
consulo, -ere, -ui, -tum. plan; consult.
contineo, -ere, -tinui, -tentum. hold together; contain, restrain.
*corona, -ae, f. wreath.
corpus, -oris, n. body.
cotidie (adv.). daily.
credo, -ere, -credidi, creditum. believe; entrust.
cum (prep. w. abl.). with.
cupio, -ere, -ii, -itum. desire.
cur. (adv.). why.
cura, -ae, f. care.
curo, 1. take care, see to it; cause (to be done).
curro, -ere, cucurri, cursum. run.

cursus, -us, m. running; course.
custos, -odis, m. guard.

de (prep. w. abl.). from, down from; concerning, about; with.
debeo, -ere, debui, debitum. owe; ought.
defendo, -ere, defendi, defensum. defend.
defero, -ferre, -tuli, -latum. carry down or away; report; bestow.
defessus, -a, -um. tired, exhausted.
deligo, -ere, -legi, -lectum. choose, select.
derideo, -ere, -si, -sum. to laugh at, scoff at, deride.
desero, -ere, -serui, -sertum. abandon, desert.
desisto, -ere, -stiti, -stitum. cease.
deus, -i, m. god.
dexter, -tera, -terum. right (hand).
dico, -ere, dixi, dictum. say, tell.
*dictum, -i, n. word.
dies, -ei, m. (f.). day.
dignus, -a, -um. worthy.
diu. (adv.). a long time.
do, dare, dedi, datum. give.
doleo, -ere, dolui, dolitum. grieve (at), be pained.
domus, -us, f. house, home.
dubito, 1. doubt; hesitate.
duco, -ere, duxi, ductum. lead.
*dudum. (adv.). just now.
dum (conj.). while; until.
duo, duae, duo. two.
durus, -a, -um. hard.

*ecastor. (exclamation). by Castor!
*eccam = ecce eam. here it is.
*eccum. = ecce + eum. ecce: (demonstrative adv.). see!
*edepol. (exclamation). by Pollux!
*edo, -ere or esse, edi, esum. to eat.
efficio, -ere, -feci, -fectum. cause, effect, bring about.
emo, -ere, emi, emptum. buy; take.
enim (conj.). for; indeed.
eo, ire, -ii, iturus. go.
equidem. (adv.). truly, indeed.
equus, -i, m. horse.
*ergo. (adv.). therefore.
*erus, -i, m. master.
etiam (conj.). also; even.
ex, e (prep. w. abl.). out of, in accord with, from.
*exeo, -ire, -ii, -itum. to go out.
experior, -iri, expertus. test, try out, find.
exspecto, 1. wait for.
extra (prep. w. acc.). outside of, beyond.

facilis, -e. easy.
facio, -ere, feci, factum. make; do.
fallo, -ere, fefelli, falsum. deceive, disappoint, prove false.
fames, famis, f. hunger.

familia, -ae, f. household.
ferro, ferre, tuli, latum. bring, carry; bear, endure.
fides, -ei, f. faith, trust.
filius, -i, m. son.
finis, -is, m. limit, end; (pl.). territory.
fio, fieri, factus sum. be made, be done; become; happen.
*flagitium, -ii, n. a shameful or disgraceful thing.
*foris, -is, f. door; in pl. the two leaves of a door.
forma, -ae, f. shape; beauty; appearance.
forte (abl.). by chance.
frango, -ere, fregi, fractum. break.
frater, -tris, m. brother.
frons, -ntis, f. front; forehead.
frustra (adv.). in vain.
fugio, -ere, fugi, fugitum. flee.

*gaudeo, -ere, gavisus. to be glad.
*gemini, -ae, -a. twin.
gens, gentis, f. tribe, race, nation.
*germanus, -i, m. brother.
gero, -ere, gessi, gestum. carry; carry on, wage (war).
gratia, -ae, f. favor, influence; gratitude; thanks, no thanks.

habeo, -ere, -ui, -itum. have; consider.
*habito, 1. to live.
*haud. (adv.). not at all, by no means.
*hercle. (exclamation). by Hercules!
hic, haec, hoc. this.
*hinc. (adv.). from here.
*hodie. (adv.). today.
homo, -inis, m. man, human being.
hostis, -is, m. enemy.
huc. (adv.). hither, to this place.

iam (adv.). already; now.
ibi (adv.). there, in that place.
idem, eadem, idem. same.
*igitur. (adv.). therefore.
ignoro, 1. be ignorant.
*immo. on the contrary.
imperium, -ii, n. command, power.
impero, 1. command, order.
impetro, 1. obtain (one's request).
in (prep. w. acc.). into; against.
incendo, -ere, -cendi, -censum. burn, set fire to.
incipio, -ere, -cepi, -ceptum. begin.
inde (adv.). thence, from there, then.
indico, -ere, -dixi, -dictum. declare, proclaim.
inimicus, -i, m. (personal) enemy.
iniuria, -ae, f. wrong, injury.
in malam crucem. See line 66.
inquam (defective). say.

*insanio, -ire, -ii, -itum. to be insane.
*insanus, -a, -um. unsound in mind, mad, insane.
insidiae, -arum, f. pl. ambush; plot.
insula, -ae, f. island.
intellego, -ere, -lexi, -lectum. understand, know.
inter (prep. w. acc.). between, among.
interea (adv.). meanwhile.
interim (adv.). meanwhile.
*interrogo, 1. to ask.
intra (prep. w. acc.). within, inside of.
*intro. (adv.). within, in.
invenio, -ire, -veni, -ventum. come upon, find.
invitus, -a, -um. unwilling.
ipse, ipsa, ipsum. -self (intensive).
*iratus, -a, -um. angry.
iste, ista, istud. that (of yours).
ita (adv.). so, thus.
item (adv.). likewise.
iubeo, -ere, iussi, iussum. order.
iungo, -ere, iunxi, iunctum. join.
iuro, 1. swear, take an oath.
ius, iuris, n. right, law.

labor, -oris, m. toil, hardship.
lapis, -idis, m. stone.
latus, -eris, n. side, flank.
legio, -onis, f. legion.
levis, -e. light.
lex, legis, f. law.
liber, -era, -erum. free.
liberi, -orum, m. (pl.). children.
libero, 1. free.
licet, -ere, licuit (impers.). it is permitted, one may.
locus, -i, m. (pl. loca, -orum, n.). place.
longus, -a, -um. long.
loquor, loqui, locutus. speak, talk.
lux, lucis, f. light.

magis (adv.). more.
magnus, -a, -um. large.
malo, malle, malui. prefer.
malus, -a, -um. bad.
mando, 1. entrust; command.
maneo, -ere, mansi, mansum. remain, stay, wait, wait for.
manus, -us, f. hand, band.
mare, maris, n. sea.
mater, -tris, f. mother.
*medicus, -i, m. doctor.
medius, -a, -um. middle (of).
mens, mentis, f. mind.
mercator, -oris, m. merchant, trader.
mereo, -ere, merui, meritum. deserve, be worthy of.
*meretrix, -icis, f. courtesan.

metus, -us, m. fear.
meus, -a, -um. my, mine.
*mi = mihi.
mille (indecl.). a thousand.
milia, -ium, n. thousands.
miror, 1. wonder at, be surprised.
mirus, -a, -um. strange, wonderful.
miser, -era, -erum. wretched.
mitto, -ere, misi, missum. send.
modo (adv.). only; just now, now, lately.
modus, -i, m. manner, way, limit.
moneo, -ere, monui, monitum. warn, advise.
mora, -ae, f. delay.
moror, 1. delay.
mors, mortis, f. death.
mos, moris, m. custom, habit.
moveo, -ere, movi, motum. move.
*mox. (adv.). soon.
mulier, -eris, f. woman.
multus, -a, -um. much; (pl.). many.
munus, -eris, n. duty; function; gift.
muto, 1. change; exchange.

nam (conj.). for.
nanciscor, -i, nactus. find, obtain, get.
nascor, nasci, natus. be born.
natio, -onis, f. tribe, race, nation.
navis, -is, f. ship.
ne (conj.). that...not, lest; that.
necesse (indecl.). necessary.
nego, 1. say...not, deny.
negotium, -ii, n. business; trouble.
nemo, gen. nullius. no one.
neque (nec) (conj.). and...not, neither, nor.
neque...neque. neither...nor.
*nescio, -ire, -ii, -itum. not to know, to be ignorant.
neuter, -tra, -trum. neither.
nihil, n. nothing.
nimis. (adv.). too.
nisi (conj.). unless, if...not.
nolo, nolle, nolui. be unwilling, not wish.
nomen, -inis, n. name.
non (adv.). not.
nosco, -ere, novi, notum. become acquainted with; (perf.) know.
noster, -tra, -trum. our, ours.
novus, -a, -um. new.
nox, noctis, f. night.
nullus, -a, -um. no, not one.
num (adv.). whether; (used also in questions expecting a negative
          answer).
numerus, -i, m. number.
numquam (adv.). never.

nunc (adv.). now.
nuntio, 1. announce.
nuntius, -ii, m. messenger; message.

ob (prep. w. acc.). on account of.
obsecro, 1. to beg, ask.
obtineo, -ere, -tinui, -tentum. hold; occupy.
occasio, -onis, f. opportunity.
occido, -ere, occidi, occisum. kill.
occupo, 1. seize.
octo. eight.
oculus, -i, m. eye.
omnis, -e. all, every.
opera, -ae, f. effort; services.
oportet, -ere, oportuit (impers.). it behooves; (one) ought.
oppidum, -i, n. town.
opprimo, -ere, -pressi, -pressum. crush, overwhelm.
opus, -eris, n. work.
opus (est). (there is) need of + abl.
ordo, -inis, m. row; rank; arrangement; order.
oro, 1. pray, beg.
*ostium, -i, n. door.

*palla, -ae, f. a woman's mantle.
par, paris. equal.
*parasitus, -i, m. parasite, sponger.
parco, -ere, peperci, parsum. spare.
paro, 1. prepare.
pars, partis, f. part.
parvus, -a, -um. small.
passus, -us, m. pace.
pateo, -ere, patui. extend; be open.
pater, -tris, m. father.
patior, pati, passus. allow, permit; suffer.
pauci, -ae, -a. few.
pecunia, -ae, f. money.
pendo, -ere, pependi, pensum. hang; pay; weigh; consider.
per (prep. w. acc.). through, by.
pereo, -ire, perii, peritum. perish.
periculum, -i, n. danger.
perspicio, -ere, -spexi, -spectum. perceive, see through, see (clearly).
pes, pedis, m. foot.
peto, -ere, -ii, -itum. seek; beg.
*phrygio, -onis, m. embroiderer.
placeo, -ere, -ui, -itum. please.
polliceor, -eri, pollicitus. promise.
pono, -ere, posui, positum. put, put down, place, pitch (camp).
populus, -i, m. people, nation.
porta, -ae, f. gate, door.
portus, -us, m. harbor.
posco, -ere, poposci. demand.
possum, posse, potui. be able, can.
post (prep. w. acc. or adv.). after; behind.

postea (adv.). afterward.
postquam (conj.). after.
postulo, 1. demand.
*poto, 1. to drink.
praebeo, -ere, -ui, -itum. furnish; offer; show.
praeda, -ae, f. booty.
*praedico, 1. to say, state, declare.
praesens, -entis. present.
praesidium, -ii, n. guard, garrison; protection.
praeterea (adv.). besides, furthermore.
*prandium, -ii, n. lunch.
primus, -a, -um. first.
prior, -ius. former.
prius (adv.). before.
priusquam (conj.). before.
pro (prep. w. abl.). before; for, in exchange for, on behalf of.
*pro. (interjection). O!
procul (adv.). afar, at a distance.
proelium, -ii, n. battle.
prohibeo, -ere, -hibui, -hibitum. prevent.
prope (adv.). near, nearly.
propter (prep. w. acc.). on account of.
propterea (adv.). for this reason.
puer, pueri, m. boy.

quaero, -ere, quaesii, quaesitum. seek; ask.
*quaeso, -ere, -ii. to beg, pray, ask.
quam (adv.). how; as; than.
*quando. (conj.). since.
quantus, -a, -um. how great, how much, (as great) as.
quattuor. four.
*quia. (conj.). because.
quicumque, quaecumque, quodcumque. whoever, whichever, whatever.
quidam, quaedam, quiddam (or quoddam). (a) certain (one).
quidem (adv.). indeed, certainly, at least.
quin (conj.). but that, that; from; why...not.
quis, quid. who? what?
quisquam, quicquam (or quidquam). anyone, anything.
quisque, quaeque, quidque (or quodque). each, each one.
*quisquis, quaeque, quicquid. whoever, whatever.
quo (adv.). whither, to which place.
quod (conj.). because; (as to) the fact that, that.
*quom = cum.
quoniam (conj.). since.
quoque (conj.). also.

rapio, -ere, rapui, raptum. snatch.
ratio, -onis, f. reckoning, plan, reason; manner.
*recte. (adv.). rightly, properly.
reddo, -ere, reddidi, redditum. return, give back; render.
redeo, -ire, -ii, -itum. return, go back.
*refero, -ferre, rettuli, relatum. to bring back.

regio, -onis, f. region, direction.
regnum, -i, n. royal power; kingdom.
relinquo, -ere, reliqui, relictum. leave behind, abandon.
repente (adv.). suddenly.
reperio, -ire, repperi, repertum. find, find out.
res, rei, f. thing, matter, affair.
respondeo, -ere, -spondi, -sponsum. answer, reply.
rex, regis, m. king.
rogo, 1. ask.
rursus (adv.). again, in turn.

saepe (adv.). often.
salus, -utis, f. safety; greetings.
*salve. (imperative) Health! Greetings!
*salvus, -a, -um. saved, preserved, safe, well, sound.
*sanus, -a, -um. sound in mind, sane.
satis (adv.). enough, sufficiently.
scio, -ire, scivi, scitum. know.
scribo, -ere, scripsi, scriptum. write.
sed (conj.). but.
semper (adv.). always.
sententia, -ae, f. opinion; vote.
sentio, -ire, sensi, sensum. feel, perceive, think.
septimus, -a, -um. seventh.
sequor, -i, secutus. follow.
servo, 1. save, guard, serve.
servus, -i, m. slave, servant.
sextus, -a, -um. sixth.
si (conj.). if.
sic (adv.). so, thus.
sicut (sicuti) (adv.). as if, just as.
signum, -i, n. sign, signal; standard; statue.
silva, -ae, f. forest.
similis, -e. like, similar.
simul (adv.). at the same time.
simulo, 1. pretend.
sine (prep. w. abl.). without.
singuli, -ae, -a. one at a time, one each.
socius, -ii, m. ally, associate.
sol, solis, m. sun.
*soleo, -ere, -itus. to be used or accustomed to.
solus, -a, -um. only, alone.
specto, 1. look at.
spero, 1. hope, hope for.
spes, -ei, f. hope.
*spinter, -eris, n. bracelet.
sto, stare, steti, statum. stand.
*stulte. (adv.). foolishly.
sum, esse, fui, futurum. be.
sumo, -ere, sumpsi, sumptum. take, assume.
superior, -ius. higher; former; better.
summus, -a, -um. highest; greatest.

supero, 1. conquer; surpass.
supersum, -esse, -fui, -futurum. remain over; survive.
*surripio, -ere, -rupui, -ruptum. to snatch or take away, to steal.
suspicor, 1. suspect.
sustineo, -ere, -tinui, -tentum. withstand; hold up, sustain.

*taceo, -ere, -cui, -citum. to be silent.
tam (adv.). so, so very.
tamen (conj.). nevertheless.
tantus, -a, -um. so great, so much.
tempus, -oris, n. time.
teneo, -ere, tenui, tentum. hold, keep.
tergum, -i, n. back, rear.
terra, -ae, f. earth, land.
timeo, -ere, timui. fear.
tollo, -ere, sustuli, sublatum. lift, raise; remove, take away.
trado, -ere, tradidi, traditum. hand over; transmit, hand down.
tres, tria. three.
*tristis, -e. sad, sorrowful, unhappy.
tum (adv.). then.
tuus, -a, -um. your, yours.

ubi (conj. and adv.). when; where, in which place.
ullus, -a, -um. any.
ultro (adv.). besides; voluntarily, automatically.
umquam (adv.). ever.
unde (adv.). whence, from which place.
unus, -a, -um. one, only, alone.
urbs, urbis, f. city.
*usquam. (adv.). ever.
usque (ad). as far as, all the way (to), continually.
usus, -us, m. use; experience.
usu est. there is need.
ut, uti (conj.). that; as, when.
uter, utra, utrum. which (of two).
uterque, utraque, utrumque. both, each.
utor, uti, usus. use + abl.
uxor, -oris, f. wife.

valeo, -ere, valui, valitum. be strong, be well.
vel (conj.). or; even. vel...vel: either...or.
venio, -ire, veni, ventum. come.
*verbum, -i, n. word.
*vero. (adv.). truly, indeed.
verus, -a, -um. true.
vester, -tra, -trum. your, yours.
vestis, -is, f. clothing.
via, -ae, f. road, way.
video, -ere, vidi, visum. see; passive -- seem.
vir, viri, m. man; husband.
vis, vim, vi, f. force, violence; (pl.) strength.
vita, -ae, f. life.

vivo, -ere, vixi, victum. live.
vivus, -a, -um. alive, living.
vix (adv.). scarcely.
voco, 1. call.
volo, velle, volui. wish, be willing.
voluntas, -atis, f. wish; good-will.

Made in the USA
Lexington, KY
21 November 2019